Candle Magick
a Guide for the Novice

J.E. Auer

ISBN 1-57353-110-3

Third Printing 1999

EPB-AW-110
an
ESCHATON BOOK
from

E.SCHATON™
P R O D U C T I O N S , I N C .
60 East Chestnut Street, #236
Chicago, IL 60611-2012

Write to request our current catalog!

Visit Eschaton on the Web:
http://www.eschatonbooks.com

TABLE OF CONTENTS

PREFACE

by
Ed Hubbard

Go ahead, light a candle. See what happens ...

Watch it burn, watch it dance. It moves to a rhythm like a heartbeat of its own - as if it were alive. Watch the shadows retreat from its golden light. Feel the warmth that it creates.

Now - that is magic!

The flame has been sacred since before there were candles. Most of the people of the Earth through most of their history have used oil lamps - liquid candles if you would. These also were sacred, and used in most of the same ways candles still are today - as an essential ingredient of many magical spells.

Before oil lamps there were fires, round which our ancient ancestors gathered for warmth and light, to cook and to weave magic of their own.

This book gives you the basic concepts to awaken the ability to use your natural magic. The author, J.E. Auer, presents candle magic using a wide spectrum of beliefs and tools that you can use to enrich your life, doing this in an easy and understandable way.

According to the Vangello delle Streghe, the Gospel of the Italian witches, the great goddess Diana existed alone and in darkness - her spirit floating in a vast and moonless sea of night before the first creation. Then Diana created the first act of magic, separating herself into two parts, she created the God - the lord of light and fire. Thus, she created the light out of herself, lit the first fire in an act of primordial creation remembered as the big bang when a billion points for fire exploded from a single spot to drift into the universe as billion suns, their fallout cooling to form planets, asteroids, etc....

In this way, every time you light a candle you are repeating the first act of creation.

The author provides you with introductory steps toward building your magical imagination, an opening to your creative self. By working with the hidden forces, with candles and with incantations, you can take control over your life and your destiny. This book gives you the tools to cast spells like a witch.

It is the nature of fire to transform. Consuming its fuel, fire transforms solid matter to energy, light and heat. When applied with care, it transforms raw foods to cooked, mud to brick, ore to metalwork. This too, is magic.

It is this power of transformation to which we appeal, and what we seek to emulate with candle magic. It is a powerful charm, for it lays at the heart of the universe. The very nature of existence - in this world at least.

From the very moment of primordial creation, physical existence has been about transformation of glowing molten matter and gases into suns and worlds. Transformation of molecules into cells, cells into animals, simple amoebas into creatures of surpassing complexity. More importantly for the spirit, it is the process of transforming emotion into thought and thought into existence.

Wow!, that's heavy!!!

J.E. Auer's book explains how to do easy, basic rituals that can be as simple or as complicated as you desire. The method is flexible, practical and widely used by many people.

In one afternoon's reading - you could be ready to cast your first ritual. Auer covers the seven ancient planets, the workings of the moon, and bringing love and healing into your living room. The secrets held silent for so long are now expertly presented for the reading public.

But will Candle Magic work for me?

By practicing the principles in this book, you can and will bring results. The magic you discover in this book will transform your life. For some, candle magic is a form of focusing on their goals, to clarify their daily lives. To set aside a time to contemplate and consciously strive for their goals. For others it is a way to discover and direct hidden psychic talents. Whatever your reasons are for using candle magic, this book will be an invaluable resource.

You will never look at a candle the same way again. Enjoy ...

DEDICATION

For my parents.

INTRODUCTION

The Candle

Barbara Walker, in her book *The Woman's Dictionary of Symbols and Sacred Objects*, identifies candles as some of the oldest elements in religious ritual. The small flames shining persistently in the darkness, she observes, could symbolize the immortality of the soul, shining on in the darkness of death. Several authors on the subject of candle magic observe that most of us have performed a candle magic ritual because that is basically what wishing while blowing out the candles on a birthday cake is! To me, candles seem to be a natural magical symbol because they are not just light but flame. Before science revealed the processes by which fire is produced, it seemed to manifest from nothing - a potentially powerful substance where seemingly nothing had been. To light a candle is to call forth power from nothing.

And we must not forget that the fire of the candle is a source of light. Light characterizes the condition of being alert, visionary and awake. Darkness characterizes unconsciousness - the state of being asleep or unaware, the condition of being hidden. I remember being told that some Orthodox Christians speak of their icons as being "asleep" when they are in shadow and "awake" when illuminated. In modern science, light is the fastest thing known - an unmatchable standard by which other things are measured. It is the purest of energies, the least encumbered by matter. It is at the very edge of mundane existence. In the Jewish and Christian creation myth, light is the first element of creation, called forth by the voice of God. "Let there be light." The Jewish Qabalists made the behavior of this first light the object of a highly developed mystical system. To light a candle is to renew creation. Still, as Leo Vinci points out in *The Practical Book of Candle Magic*, the Christian Church did not always look favorably in the earliest days on the use of candles in worship. Many leaders in the Early Church considered the use of candles to be a "heathen" practice. It was impossible, however, to long repress the use of one of the oldest methods of creating an atmosphere of spirituality and reverence for the sacred.

It is a good thing, I think, to begin these operations with a meditation on light - its pure and glorious illumination. Imagine it bathing you, warming you and strengthening, awakening and revealing the noblest and truest part of your nature.

The Craft of Magic

What is magic? First, is magic a religion? It can be. But for our purposes here magic is a craft. It is the practice of using certain tools to create something of use. Like all crafts, magic may be used both for spiritual development and as a means to be of service to one's community.

There are several classic definitions of magic. For my purposes, I would describe magic first simply as a manipulation of reality. The important issue, really, is whether it is a manipulation of interior or exterior reality. The fact is that we live in a skeptical age and it is impossible to determine what would have happened if a spell had never been cast. We cannot tell if a magical operation has actually altered the course of events in some way. We cannot tell if all it does is alter one's perceptions so as to make one more receptive to and better aware of the forces operating in one's life. However, if that really is all magic does, then there is still a lot to be said for it - perhaps more to be said for it than if it were simply a means of "getting your own way" or "getting the upper hand."

For this reason, I would caution people reading this book against putting too much emphasis on tangible results. Instead, concentrate on working with the hidden connection between seemingly unrelated things - between, for example, planetary energies, colors, the fragrances of plants, letters of the alphabet, numbers, geometric shapes, the pictures on Tarot cards etc. Modern occultist Gareth Knight in his book *Magic and the Western Mind* speaks of "the magical imagination" and calls magic "a high art and science... that should release the powers of the imagination for the benefit of any other part of life."

Now this little manual is not intended to teach advanced spiritual disciplines or esoteric sciences. However, I would like to think that it will provide a few small introductory steps toward building the magical imagination. The idea, in my interpretation, is not so much to gain the ability to direct the world around you but to create a resonance between you and the complex interlacing of hidden forces beneath the mundane world and so gain greater harmony with the world around you. You may, indeed, gain the ability to exert more influence on the events in your life. Or it may be that you will simply become better able to receive the good life offers you and better able to respond to the challenges that life brings you. You should be able to focus the benefits into specific aspects of your life and toward specific challenges.

Knight observes that every act of perception is a creative, imaginative act because our minds must structure the things that we perceive in order to work with them. The mind creates the world as we know it through this process. Beyond that, our imaginations fuse images and concepts together so that they transcend their mundane significance. To change the way our minds order and perceive the world, therefore, is no small transformation. Some would even go so far as to say that internal and external reality are not as separate as we are in the habit of thinking and that when we change the way we perceive reality, it actually effects a change on reality. I will not venture here to say with certainty if the process we call "magic" is external or purely internal. My guess would be that it is a combination of both - and perhaps more one thing for some than it is for others. The great modern psychological theorist, Carl Gustav Jung, divided the world between introverted and extroverted people. Perhaps there is introverted and extroverted magic as well?

Anyway, if we could not assume magic to have some kind external effect - if we assumed that it could only effect the consciousness of the person performing the ritual - it would be futile to attempt to perform magical operations on behalf of other people or on behalf of the community in which one lives. My experience tends to be that things really do seem to "happen" - but not necessary exactly as planned. Problems do resolve themselves and there is a general feeling of energy being released. It is, however, far less directed than one might expect. The idea that the way we perceive the world in fact shapes the world to some extent is truly something to ponder. We come into harmony with the world and the world comes into greater resonance with us and, if we cultivate self-knowledge, perhaps even into resonance with our most profound motivations and purposes.

Creating harmony where there was disharmony, is, of course, a healing act. And this, of course, is an act of service to the world around you, to the community in which you live. Furthermore, the sort of magic that we are discussing here uses some fairly mundane objects - candles, perhaps some herbs from the kitchen. This has the great advantage of bringing the magical dimension into ordinary life and strengthening the sense of mystical connection between all things, even the most humble and everyday things.

Christian Magic?

It is not my intention here to create a collection of Christian spells or outline a magical tradition that should be identified as character-istically Christian. However, if you study candle rituals from other sources, one thing that might surprise and puzzle you would be all the Christian elements. There are frequently bibles placed on one corner of the ritual altar. The recitation of psalms is often central to the ritual. Raymond Buckland in *Practical Candleburning Rituals* refers to the "customary" use of certain psalms and other biblical passages with candle rituals to achieve certain purposes - texts that sometimes have no clear relationship to the purpose of the spell. This indicates to me that there is a tradition behind the use of these specific scriptural passages in these rituals that is so old that the logic behind their selection has been completely obscured. Buckland, unfortunately, is rather vague about the history of the practices he has collected, preferring to concentrate instead on the practical aspects of candle rituals. Other sources refer to Christian concepts like the Holy Spirit.

As I said, this combination of Christianity and magic may at first seem puzzling. Since about 1980, we have been conditioned to consider Christianity and occultism as opposite things. With the rise of the Religious Right here in the United States, non-Christian occultists were constantly confronted by vocal Christian reactionaries condemning their activities. Christian occultists were, meanwhile, under constant pressure to choose between Christianity and occultism. Many decided that they could no longer in good conscience continue occult practices. Others decided that they could no longer remain in the Church if their freedom of spiritual inquiry was going to be restricted. Christian occultists became rare. Still, one only has to look at things like the work of Dion Fortune (*Psychic Self-Defense, Meditations on the Collects*) and the anonymous *Meditations on the Tarot* to see that Christianity and occultism were not always assumed to be strange bedfellows.

To be sure, there are Biblical pronouncements against magical practices. The Old Testament pronouncements seem to mostly have to do with two things: practices that many other primitive cultures condemn (like necromancy) and the Israelite's desire to purge their religious life of superficial ritual - especially, but hardly exclusively - the practices of their polytheistic pagan neighbors. (How many people, reading these Old Testament texts, realize that Jewish folklore is full of tales of wonder working wise men? Their supernatural abilities, however, were not cultivated for their own sake but were considered a sign of wisdom and holiness.) The New Testament writers may simply pick up the distrust of sorcerers that seems to have been common in the Graeco-Roman world at that time. Such people were considered charlatans and con men - rather like televangelists today.

The definition of what constitutes magic can often be tricky. I might characterize my view of the world as "science and religion" and dismiss yours as "magical superstition and quackery." In times when supernaturalism was more prevalent, I might call the wonder workers of my culture "prophets" and dismiss the ones from yours as merely "skilled in magical artifice." The Old Testament condemns "diviners", yet Joseph tells fortunes by interpreting dreams, and the prophet Samuel seems to have started out as a paid soothsayer. The question seems to have been one of just whose "diviners" they were! As we move into the early Christian period, we find what we would call "healing rituals" routinely used by doctors, just as they had been in pre-Christian antiquity. My impression is that one couldn't, in many eras, practice medicine in a credible way without resorting to what we now would call "magic". Indeed, as late as the 17th century, the English believed that wood from a young ash tree, pruned just as the Sun entered the sign of Taurus, would cure a nose-bleed. King James II himself was reported to have successfully undergone such a cure. Today, that sounds like magic but, back then, it was considered medicine not witchery. The cure was administered by a surgeon who was remembered for his cleverness. Witchcraft, on the other hand, continued to be condemned. Indeed, just a few years later, the good people of Salem, Massachusetts would hang a couple dozen of their neighbors because they suspected them of witchcraft. Clearly, the King's cure was considered to be something else. Consider also: when a Medieval farmer buried a consecrated host to insure a good harvest or "baptized" his cattle to protect them, did he consider that "magic", "religion" or just good agriculture?

More importantly, it becomes apparent that the practice of magic often functioned among the lower classes as a means of compensating for the social powerlessness they felt - it gave them what they believed to be the means to protect themselves from abuse and to avenge wrongs committed against them, even if the established legal authorities proved indifferent to their grievances. Those who are used to the modern witch's "harm none" ethic would be quite shocked by the often harsh and aggressive character of many traditional peasant spells. Buckland, in his book on candle magic, even distinguishes the folk practices he collected from "witchcraft" because he felt the hurtful character of some of the spells was inconsistent with the ethical system that is essential to his definition of witchcraft. At any rate, whatever such folk practices may have actually been able to do to relieve people's problems, they made common folk feel less helpless. This is probably a feature of folk magical practices in many societies, regardless of religion. It would have been present not only in non-Christian societies but also in the peasant societies of Medieval Christian Europe.

Indeed, perhaps this was part of the thinking behind the European witch hunts. Stamping out the magic of the common folk was a way of keeping them in their places. Accusing someone of "black magic" was a way of suggesting that he did not know his place. Perhaps this is why the methods the witch hunters used seemed to better lend themselves to rounding up and condemning people who had somehow violated established social boundaries (especially gender boundaries) than they did to determining who was actually engaging in magical practices or pagan rituals.

Planetary Magic

Although I hope to include some folk practices in this manual, the planetary system used in this book specifically seems to derive from occult traditions of the Renaissance period. Knight reports that Renaissance occultists broke the world, in neat Aristotelian fashion, into a three-tiered system. There was the earth (which they then imagined to be the center of the cosmos) and there was heaven, where God and the angels dwelt and governed the affairs of the world. Between heaven and earth was the realm of the celestial spheres: the "planetary bodies". The angels caused the "planetary bodies" to move and the "planetary bodies" in turn exerted their influences over the human affairs. Each of the seven "planets" - the planets that were then known but also the Sun and the Moon - each represented a particular type of cosmic influence. It is perhaps from this tradition that we came to speak of people as being "mercurial" (after the planet Mercury) or "jovial" (after the planet Jupiter) or "saturnine" (after the planet Saturn). "Lunatics", also, were people thought to be held in fascination by the illusions which the Moon's influence was believed to generate. At the time, all this was believed to be a scientific analysis of the structure of the cosmos.

Of course, what we are talking about here is astrology. Today we tend to think of astrology more as a system of spiritual symbolism than a scientific description of the world's operation. The ancient science of alchemy is similar. When taken literally as science, alchemy fails completely but, at the same time, it generates a profound system of spiritual symbolism. Astrology was clearly present in Medieval Christian Europe. It was found in pagan antiquity and revived as part of the new knowledge acquired from the Islamic countries at the time of the Crusades. Opinions about astrology and astrological forces in the Middle Ages and Renaissance were surprisingly mixed. Augustine condemned it as a dangerously fatalistic superstition (the modern theological point of view, by the way) but Aquinas apparently acknowledged the influence of astrological forces in human life and felt their use for the limited purpose of taking advantage of their supposed effects on medicinal herbs and mineral compounds was entirely legitimate. The Protestant Reformers also split on the issue as did Medieval popes. Some popes piously condemned astrological practices while others consulted astrologers just as secular rulers of the time did. On the Protestant side, Luther apparently even wrote a preface for a book on astrology.

Now, Medieval and Renaissance Christianity clearly considered both magic and astrology to be questionable practices. The unfortunate astrologer Cecco D'Ascoli was burned at the stake at Florence in 1327. The great Peter of Abano died in 1316 during his second heresy trial. He had been acquitted once and it is impossible to say what the outcome here would have been had he lived to defend himself. His body, however, was burned in disgrace.

However, the Church's condemnation of these practices does not seem to be nearly as total as we have come to expect, especially as we move out of the Middle Ages and into the more adventurous Renaissance. (The city of Padua would eventually put up a statue in honor of Peter of Abano, praising his skill as an astrologer and recording that the heresy charges had been false.) How were such things possible? Well, we have to keep in mind that what we today lump all together as "supernatural phenomena" and "occult practices" in past ages were divided into several separate categories. By the Renaissance, Knight reports, it was believed that the affairs of heaven and the angelic powers that dwelt there were indeed the exclusive domain of the Church. It was, however, arguably permissible for laymen to seek to manipulate the astrological realms believed to lie between earth and heaven - to seek to control the influence of the planets. It was considered a separate area of study - part of the natural world and so was called "natural magic".

The Renaissance is an era filled with great magicians - the sinister and legendary Dr. Faust and the unfortunate Giordano Bruno (who was burned at the stake for renouncing the Christian religion in favor of what he imagined to be the true religion of ancient Egypt) as well as such important figures as John Dee and Paracelesus. It is a period of history in which the distinctions between science and religion and magic often blurred. The Renaissance magician known for developing a planetary system based on the concepts of so-called "natural magic" was Marsilio Ficino (1433-99).

Ficino seems to have spent his life in the household of the Medici in Florence. He was a priest, physician and classical scholar as well as an astrologer and philosopher of magic. It was in his capacity as a court translator of Greek that it fell to him to translate the *Hermetica* and so undertake the study of esoteric knowledge. (Although it was believed at the time to be of great antiquity, the *Hermetica* was actually a sort of blending of pagan and Christian material from the first centuries of the Christian era.) Ficino insisted that planetary influences were part of the natural world and, therefore, appropriate objects of human manipulation. His magical system depended on using the correspondences believed to exist between planetary influences and various mundane objects. Knight reports that compilations of such astrological correspondences became quite popular in this era. One of the most famous is *De Occulta Philosophia* published in 1531 by the German magician Cornelius Agrippa (1486-1535).

Ficino seemed to have felt that these techniques could be used to enhance people's physical and emotional well being. As one hears of Ficino's often elaborate procedures (involving things like singing hymns to the classical deity associated with a particular planet), it is interesting to note that Ficino's book *Liber di Vita* was published in 1489 - just three years after the infamous *Malleus Malificarum*. The inquisitiveness and relative freedom of the Renaissance scholars existed side by side which the witch hunts of the late Middle Ages.

Ficino's ideas were expanded by another Renaissance magician, the scholarly prodigy Giovanni Pico della Mirandola (1463-94). Today, Pico is probably chiefly remembered by skeptics as an early debunker of astrology. We forget that Pico was himself an astrologer and a student of Ficino. True, he challenged much of the minutia of astrology as pseudo-science but his quarrel was specifically with predictive and divinatory astrology, not with the idea that planetary forces influenced a person's emotional disposition and physical constitution. Ficino himself had also been rather skeptical of predictive astrology, apparently because it was incompatible with Christian teachings about human free will.

Knight reports, however, that Pico had other significant esoteric areas of interest. He was, essentially, the founder of the gentile tradition of interpreting the Jewish Qabala. This is where he really went beyond Ficino. (Unlike Ficino, who seems to have been purely a classical scholar, Pico was also schooled in Hebrew.) Angelic correspondences to planetary influences (apparently identical in many respects to the ones in this book) seem to have been known at least as far back as Peter of Abano in the early 14th century but manipulating those forces was a highly questionable practice, as we have seen. Pico's Qabalism included a system of working with this angelic sphere as well as the planetary sphere and so Ficino's planetary magic acquired a new layer. (Jewish lore about the extent to which it was appropriate for people to try to influence angelic activities for human benefit was somewhat different from the Christian understanding of those issues.) The limitations which Ficino imposed on his system - natural, planetary forces only, no angelic powers involved - generally succeeded in keeping him out of trouble with the Church. Pico's fortunes, however, were far more mixed. He was even imprisoned at one point. Still, surprisingly, the reaction was apparently not entirely negative - despite the fact that Pico claimed that Jesus had performed his miracles through Qabalistic principles. Knight reports that "alternate popes condemned or proclaimed his work".

The system I will be using here will describe both the planetary influences and the angelic powers traditionally associated with them. I hope I have given you a sense of the historical background against which, I suspect, the various traditions of candle burning rituals brought together here developed. It is my intention, however, to help readers work with these versatile ritual tools creatively so that they might be integrated into a variety of magical traditions rather than recreate a tradition from the past.

Magical Ethics

Before I get into actual practical techniques, I think I should discuss some ethical guidelines. Let us understand right now what this book is. It is a book for beginners whom I will never meet. For this reason, I am giving you the simplest kind of advice I can about the right and wrong of using this material.

The first principle is that you should never do anything that seems to you ethically wrong. It is just that simple. I've tried to present this material in such a way that you can use it creatively. You can add things to it and you can leave things out according to what seems right to you. However, if in reading this book, the practices outlined in it seem to you wrong on some basic level, then my advice would be for you to put it down. I have no desire to persuade you to do things against your conscience. Also, if you have a religion - whether it is Pagan or Christian or something else - I would advise you to continue to practice it and practice it faithfully. It can help shape your conscience and ethical integrity. Furthermore, if at any time you feel that you have found a spiritual path that is more fulfilling than the practice of magical rituals of the type described in this book and lose interest in this material, that is perfectly all right. I only hope that this will help you on your journey.

Second, you should do no harm. The greatest thing about the practice of magic is its ability to heal the disharmonies of our complex world. Doing harm is completely inconsistent with this. I don't mean to dismiss what we might call "warrior spirituality" - magic as a strengthening and protective force, aiding the cause of justice. However, that has nothing to do with being magically aggressive toward others. I have said that magical practices were often used as weapons by oppressed people to give them a more equitable lot in life or at least to ease their sense of powerlessness. We live in a much more fortunate age, and we are not helpless peasants; there is no excuse for using these techniques in a vindictive or controlling way. Our modern world has many opportunities for self-empowerment, if you feel that you are helpless, try doing rituals to help you draw some of them into your life.

Remember also that everything is interconnected. Taking revenge forges a connection that gives others license to take revenge on you. As you punish, so you invite judgment. One of the first things I discovered was that blessing those who oppressed me often released their hold on me and robbed their negativity of fuel. See if it works for you. (Everyone is different.) One blessing may give you more protection than ten curses.

What constitutes "harm", however, is often a judgment call. You can't always tell what negative consequences your actions will have. Some practitioners recommend doing a Tarot reading at the start of a magical operation to make sure that it is favorably aspected. More than that, however, some traditions define any attempt to control the actions of another as "harm". (And many go even farther than that and say that helping anyone by magical means who has not asked for your help is "harm" because it interferes with people's freedom of choice and robs them of an opportunity to find solutions to their own problems. I wouldn't take it quite that far but the issues involved are clearly something to think about.)

If it were strictly true that all efforts to influence another's behavior are "harm", then any magic done to help a friend heal a broken marriage or help a teen off drugs or to stop a hostile person from interfering with your life would be "harm". It seems to me that this approach is simplistic and overly restrictive. I would say, first of all, that "control" does not include heightening someone's perception of a situation - helping a couple perceive the common joys that first brought them together, helping someone's boss perceive what a good worker someone is. These things are not "harm". What I would say is that, in general, you should try to avoid doing magical work with the assumption that you know better than other people what is good for them. History is full of people with this attitude - men who knew what was good for women, Christians who knew what was good for the heathen, Romans who knew what was good for the barbarians etc. Controlling another's behavior can only be justified when it is clear that there is danger of that person doing real harm to herself or to another. Even then, you should be careful that you are not rationalizing attempts to gain power over others. Remember also, it takes time, study and work to purify your intentions and to replace your natural need to control the world around you.

I would warn you especially about love spells. Trying to make a specific person fall in love with you or someone else is a very traditional magical operation. However, it is also an extremely controlling one. It basically enslaves someone as a companion either to you or another. I tend to discourage the practice. Try instead to work on developing the attractive qualities and the openness to recognizing and receiving the love of a soul mate in the person seeking love - whether that person is you or someone else. Don't focus on controlling the affections of a specific person.

As you can see, it's a matter of judgment. As you work and develop, you will get a stronger sense of what is right for you, how best to operate within these principles and when and if exceptions can be made. This is something that comes with maturity, experience and self-knowledge. In the beginning, stick with the rules. Divination techniques like Tarot readings may help you make these decisions. They may also increase your sensitivity to the issues involved.

Finally, I think that I should note that I do feel that there is something valid behind all the traditional Christian warnings against magical practices. It is simply this: If we could be in complete control of everything that happens in our lives, we would have no challenges and no opportunity for spiritual growth. We would be spoiled little wizards, expecting the universe to always give us our way. In past ages, when magic was naively believed to yield very spectacular results, this, of course, made the whole practice highly questionable. Today, we are more sophisticated and less super-stitious and don't expect that all our problems could be solved instantly and miraculously by supernatural control. Still, the pursuit of control and the idea that lack of control constitutes failure are things which can distract you from the things which foster real spiritual development - confronting and struggling with the problems of life. Using magic to avoid such challenges is a harmful, escapist venture - even if it not in the nature of these techniques to grant you that kind of control. For this reason, I repeat that you should not focus too much on getting specific results. Focus instead on building up a sense of greater harmony and resonance with the inter-connecting forces within you and outside you. I sincerely believe these techniques will help you and others as you battle with the difficulties of life but do not seek to have magic solve everything for you.

CANDLES, OTHER EQUIPMENT AND SYMBOLISM

Equipment

Here is a list of items you will need.

Altar - Most candle magic systems use altars. Generally, the objects used in the ritual are set up on a table serving as an altar. A normal card table is a convenient size. But I've worked with just a book shelf. Ideally, you should also have enough room to walk around the altar comfortably. In order to protect your ritual from unwanted influences, it's customary to establish a protective circle around your magical work area. One of the best ways of doing this involves walking around the work area. (I'll talk about this later when I discuss designing rituals.) The size of the altar will determine how many and what size candles you will use. Candles come in many different sizes, so you will have lots of options. However, it probably is not a good idea to crowd a table top with lit candles. It is traditional to set the altar up so that you work facing the east, toward the rising sun. But this is not absolutely necessary. The altar may have any appearance that pleases you - it can be dignified and churchy or more rustic and natural.

Candles - Of course! I discuss this in detail later on. Just a safety note: **Never leave the candles burning unattended.** Take the phone off the hook while you are working. Don't work with candles when you think you might have to answer the door. You should keep a water bucket near your work area (or even a small kitchen fire extinguisher). Candle rituals are probably no more dangerous than cooking but some very tragic accidents have happened in the kitchen. It's best to be prepared for an emergency.

And I should mention that there is a whole class of candles for magical rituals that this manual is not going to cover. Those are the molded novelty candles that you might see in stores handling occult supplies. Mostly, these are articles for what we might call contemporary folk magic. Some of them look quite sinister - the black devils, for example. (Yes, they can be used for cursing people but they can also be used to exorcize evil spirits. If the candle is prepared properly and the proper ritual is performed, demonic influences are supposed to melt from your life as the candle burns and the wax melts.) The legend and lore surrounding these fascinating and curious items is a whole subject in itself.

Candle holders or dishes - Obviously, if you are using taper type candles, you will need holders for them. You can probably find inexpensive candle holders in a hardware store. There are no special requirements. However, even if you are using large flat bottomed candles that stand up easily on their own, it is still a good idea to put a dish or saucer underneath them to catch the hot wax and keep it off the table top.

Matches? - Interestingly enough, some traditions discourage the use of matches in ritual because they are "brimstone" (sulphur) and associated with evil and demonic forces. I generally like to use what we might call "the same fire" to light all the candles in the ritual. That is to say, I like to light candles from other candles as much as possible. (The same with any incense I might be using.) The process has to start somewhere, however. You may want to use a cigarette lighter rather than a match to light the first candle or light it from your stove. I don't see anything wrong with striking an occasional match, however. But you probably should not be working in such a way that you are frequently striking matches.

Incense (and incense burner) - (optional) These elements can add a great deal to the ritual. I will also give this a more detailed treatment later on.

Scented oils (for dressing candles) - Similar to incense and also optional. I will discuss this later along with the incense.

Knives - Traditionally, there are supposed to be two.
  1. Used for actually cutting things - cleaning and carving symbols in candles, for example. This is a necessary tool. Your candles should be prepared and cared for with a special knife, kept good and sharp and used only for this purpose. (Sometimes called a "bolline").
  2. (optional) Often called an "athame". This is a ritual dagger used for tracing symbols in the air - think of this as the authentic

"magic wand". Scott Cunningham in his book *Wicca: A Guide for the Solitary Practitioner* notes that such ritual daggers were thought of in ancient times as symbols of command. He seems to find their use a bit arrogant - especially in his primarily religious system where one is invoking deities. In our system, such a tool would probably be appropriate when dealing with planetary energies but inappropriate when directed at the angelic powers. So should you chose to use this tool remember that its use is directed at planetary influences only. If you are calling angelic powers as well, remember that you do not command them, you simply ask them to help - make this distinction clear especially if you are using an athame. At any rate, you may choose not trace symbols in the air as part of your rituals or you may not wish to use a knife for doing so. There is no reason, for example, why you shouldn't use a wand instead of a blade, if you like the idea of tracing symbols but, for some reason, don't care for a dagger. (Keep in mind that wands also imply command.)

Pendulum or amulet - (optional) You can swing a pendulum around the candles as a means of attracting or banishing forces. Make sure the object so used is heat and fire resistant.

Bells - (optional) You can ring a bell (three times seems good) when causing an influence to manifest. Basically, this would be whenever you identify something as representing a person or a planetary influence in the course of the ritual.

Snuffer - (optional) Some think it disrespectful to blow a ritual candle out and prefer to use a snuffer.

Aloe Vera Plant - an herbal treatment for minor burns. Break a piece off and rub it on the burn. (The plant is sacred to the Moon, by the way.)

Religious statues - (optional) May be placed in the center of the altar toward the back. Incense, if used, is usually placed in front of it.

Candles

Setting Up the Candles

I'm trying to present the system that I am describing in a creative way that will leave you lots of options. It can be used to create both simple and very complex magical rituals. I want you to have the freedom to choose. Generally, I will describe things in a very complex form and detail as many possibilities as possible. You are, of course, free to modify this information and simplify the procedures to suit your own personal preferences. It is my hope that you will.

The full set up involves a sanctuary candle, altar candles and the colored candles you will use to represent the various forces operating in the ritual.

The sanctuary candle is the candle that you use to establish the sacred space in which you are working. It should be a white candle (or of a color of personal significance to you, but never black.) Long burning "24 hour" candles (large candles in glass jars) or other long burning candles work well for this. If you use this type of candle, you want to use the same candle over the course of several rituals, as sort of a constant element in your work. It isn't necessary to have this candle burning all the time - in fact, I advise against leaving candles burning unattended - but when this candle burns low, you should light its successor the first time from its flame. You can put the sanctuary candle on a second table to one side of the table you are using as an altar.

The altar candles traditionally establish the basic orientation of your work. Occultists today generally think of "black" and "white" magic distinctions as rather naive and, quite rightly, point out that these categories don't take into account the positive aspects of night and darkness. However, we still find this distinction in many candle magic traditions. Since our basic orientation is toward protection and healing rather than dominance of others, we are doing what might be called "white magic". The altar candles, if you decide to use them, by this reasoning, should be white. Usually there are two and they are often larger than the other candles used in the ritual. They are placed on either side of the rear of the area where you are working whether you set up a table to serve as an altar or not. Those working from Pagan or Wiccan traditions may prefer, instead, to have the two candles each be a different color - representing the Goddess and the God - the union of cosmic opposites. Some traditional Goddess/God color pairs are green/red or silver/gold.

Then, of course, there are the candles you use to represent the forces you are trying to influence and the people on whose behalf you are working. As I've said, the system we will be using is based on planetary influences.

The Planetary System

The planetary system that I outline here seems clearly inspired by the planetary systems of Renaissance occultists like Marsilio Ficino. It should not, however, be taken as an exact recreation of their methods. Unfortunately, I have never had the opportunity to study any of this material directly. I have not been able to determine whether using colored candles to manifest the influence of the various "planets" was a real Renaissance practice. It certainly is consistent with the tradition, however. In order to make specific planetary influences or combinations of such influences manifest in someone's life, Ficino and others like him composed hymns to the planets, gathered flowers and herbs associated with planetary influences and used metals associated with the desired influences. Knight reports that Botticelli's Renaissance masterpiece, *Venus*, may have been painted in order to strengthen the magical influence of that planet. Using colored candles to help activate specific planetary influences is certainly not very far removed from this approach. Virtually every book on candle ritual, furthermore, offers some sort of system relating the colors of the candles to astrological concepts - sometimes to planets and often to the signs of the zodiac.

The color correspondences given here are based on different systems I have encountered over the years and on what I personally have become accustomed to using. I think that I should mention that I have never seen two systems that were exactly the same. If you do your own research, you will come across additional and alternate colors associated with various things - planetary influences and other types of energies. If you feel more comfortable with them, I certainly encourage you to use them either as modifications or additions to the system below or to create your own system. And I should mention that there are several occult color systems besides this astrological one. There are Qabalistic systems and systems based on aura reading or the chakras. As you work and learn, you may find yourself influenced by these other traditions.

The angelic correspondences for the seven traditional planetary influences are standard and found in many sources. Corresponden-ces for the outer planets come specifically from a classic work on candle magic to which I owe a great deal of information about candle rituals and planetary magic: Leo Vinci's *Practical Book of Candle Magic*.

The seven planets known to the ancients were: the Sun, the Moon, Mercury, Venus, Mars, Jupiter and Saturn. (No Earth? Well, we were on Earth. Back then, we couldn't tell it was just another planet! In fact, it was considered heretical at one time to suggest that Earth was merely a planet and not the center of the universe. Neither did we know how very different the Sun and the Moon were from the other heavenly bodies we now think of as planets.) Barbara Walker mentions that, in the ancient Middle East, the Seven Veils of Ishtar were equated with these seven known "planets". So much of candle ritual seems to be of Christian origin or heavily Christianized, that Pagan readers may be interested to hear that when we talk of the "seven planets" we are in fact talking of seven keys to revealing the Great Goddess. These seven planets were eventually assigned ruler-ship of the twelve signs of the zodiac. Except for the Sun and the Moon, they each were given two signs to rule. Each planet came to be traditionally associated with an angelic power.

Later the three "outer planets" were discovered: Uranus, Neptune and Pluto. This complicated matters a little. Did they also rule signs of the zodiac? Each of the three "new" planets was eventually assigned a zodiac sign to rule. And they were also associated with "angelic powers". This gives you an option. You can use the old fashioned "seven rulers" model or you can use the modern method which adds the outer planets and their associated angels as secondary rulers.

The Planets and their Attributes

I'm going to present a great deal of information here all at once. I'll break the following list down into more workable components a little later. Since we are taking a creative approach, however, I would like you to get an overview of all the principles involved.

Here are some helpful things to keep in mind:

As I have said, planets generally rule two signs of the zodiac - sometimes with an outer planet with a co-ruler for one, sometimes not. Except for Venus, however, planetary influences are more strongly associated with the attributes of one of the signs they rule. I have identified which one that is on the guide below.

On the guide below, all the signs of the zodiac that have an outer planet as their secondary ruler are marked with an asterisk (*).

The Sun
Sign: Leo
Color - Orange, Gold or Red
Angel: Michael.
> Vitality, success, rank, strength, courage, recognition, protection, victory, soldiers, police, warrior spirituality, valiant self-sacrifice, cosmic order, activity, masculinity

Notes: With Mars' Aries energy, the Sun becomes more associated with virility. With Jupiter's Sagittarian energy, it becomes more associated with rank or status.

The Moon
Sign: Cancer
Angel: Gabriel
Color - White, Pale Blue or Silver
> Intuition, dreams, emotion, mystery, confusion, obscurity, domesticity, motherhood, cyclical phenomena, mutability, fluids, repose, passivity, femininity

Mercury
Signs: Gemini and Virgo
Angel: Raphael
Colors - Pale Yellow (as Gemini) or
         Golden Yellow or Beige (as Virgo)

As Gemini - Communication, messages, reason, the intellect, speed, youth, skill.

As Virgo - Technical skill, manual dexterity, detailed matters, anxiety, everyday management, innocence, purity, allergies and minor illnesses.

Notes: In combination with virtually any other planet, Mercury's Gemini influence generally works to speed things up. (Mercury's influence is most commonly associated with Gemini's attributes.)

Venus

Signs: Taurus and Libra

Angel: Anael

Colors - Green (as Taurus) or pink (as Libra)

As Taurus - Abundance, fertility, natural balance, prosperity, luxury, health, stamina, sensuality.

As Libra - Love, friendship, sociability, cooperation, fairness, sex.

Notes: Venus' Libran energy is commonly paired with Mars' Aries energy for love spells. The tendency of Venus' Taurean aspects to provide prosperity becomes very specifically financial when combined with Jupiter's influence. (Venus' influence is most commonly associated with both Taurus' and Libra's attributes.)

Mars

Angel: Zamael

Signs: Aries and Scorpio*

Colors - Deep Red (as Aries), Dark Red, Grey or Black (as Scorpio*)

Please see notes below on the problems associated with working with black candles.

As Aries - Anger, war, battlefields, aggression, strife, daring, protection, revenge, sexual passion, especially male sexuality and masculinity, machismo, bravado.

As Scorpio* - Sex (especially if somehow illicit or depraved), death, secrets, intrigue, hidden things, occult powers, inheritance, buried treasure. (Secondary planetary ruler for Scorpio: Pluto. Angel: Azrael)

Notes: Commonly paired with Venus for love spells. Please see notes below on problems associated with working with Mars. (Mars' influence is most commonly associated with Aries' attributes.)

Jupiter

Angel: Sachiel

Signs: Sagittarius and Pisces*

Colors - Purple or Royal Blue (as Sagittarius),
          Aqua or Marine Colors (as Pisces*)

As Sagittarius - Abundance, increase, good luck, achievement, authority, government, justice (especially in legal matters), optimism.

As Pisces* - Visions, psychic power, illusions, the sea, confusion, vague, obscure or unformed things, fake or disguised things, sexual dysfunction, alcoholism, addictions, bad habits and self destructive attitudes, anonymous or unrecognized charity or self sacrifice.

(Secondary planetary ruler for Pisces: Neptune. Angel: Asariel)

Notes: Jupiter's Sagittarian energy tends specifically to increase something you all ready have. An important warning: Jupiter's tendency to increase things is not good for things like weight loss or healing energy for a cancer patient. (Jupiter's influence is most commonly associated with Sagittarius' attributes.)

Saturn

Angel: Cassiel

Signs: Capricorn and Aquarius*

Colors - Dark Blue/Indigo, Dark Green or Black (as Capricorn),
        Electric Blue (as Aquarius)

Please see notes below on the problems associated with working with black candles.

As Capricorn - Limitations, conclusions, permanence, old age, death, slowing down, longevity, cosmic justice, fate, decrease, austerity, finding lost objects, uncovering secrets.

As Aquarius* -Revolution, change, groups of friends and comrades, clubs, teams.

(Alternate planetary ruler for Aquarius: Uranus. Angel: Uriel.)

Notes: In combination with virtually any other planet, Saturn's Capricorn influence generally works to slow things down. It is also used specifically to cause something to decrease or to put limits on something. (Saturn's influence is most commonly associated with Capricorn's attributes.)

How to Use This Information

First, you must decide if you are going to work with seven planets (the original seven, including the Sun and the Moon, known to the ancients) or if you are going to work with the modern ten planet system, (including the outer planets). I find that it is best to concentrate on the seven planets of the ancients. (In the Renaissance it was believed that these seven principles encompassed every aspect of human life.) The outer planets are secondary, to be used when nothing else will do. Thus, I would use the ancient system but not be overly rigid about it. You will probably find that you do not really need the outer planets all that often because they tend to duplicate principles represented by the more traditional planets. (Compare Neptune and the Moon, for example.) Pluto's associations with funerals, death and depraved sex and Neptune's associations with the sea, addiction and impotence are fairly unique to those planets. But how often are you really going to use them? They are useful mostly as representations of negative forces in banishing rituals but in practice, you are more likely to be concerned with more general matters like healing, protection and success.

As I've said, the guide above provides a lot of information all at once. Most of it will probably be helpful to know, especially if you desire greater flexibility in designing rituals. Generally, I would focus on the traditional seven ancient planets and the very basic principles they represent. Eventually, you may, wish to do things differently. You may wish, for example, to add a greater range of candle colors to your rituals in order to represent more specific things. The material on pages 21-23 will help you do this. For now, however, I will break the system down for you into the information you are most likely to use.

In practice, the candles representing the planetary influences with their angelic powers will be the candles that you choose in order to focus the type of energies - love, prosperity, courage etc. - that you wish to draw on. But how do you identify the people whom you wish the ritual to effect? You do this by means of their astrological signs. If you look at the planetary information presented on the last few pages, you will see that, for example, both Libra and Taurus are ruled by Venus. This makes both Libran pink and Taurean green a possibility when working with Venus energy. But it also means that you would use the color pink to signify a Libra person and the color green to signify a Taurus person. If you don't know the person's astrological sign, simply select a color that you associate with the person (e.g. red for your niece's red hair, dark blue for your boss' navy suit). Or, better yet, choose the color for an astrological sign that you feel somehow embodies qualities that you associate with that person.

The Seven Ancient Planets

The Sun (*Michael*) - Orange, Gold (or Red) candle for matters of victory, vitality, health and courage. Also virility (especially with Mars) and status (especially with Jupiter).

The Moon (*Gabriel*) - White, Pale Blue or Silver candle for matters of intuition, imagination, mystery, mutability, femininity.

Mercury (*Raphael*) - Pale Yellow candle for matters of comm-unication, the intellect, speed, youth, skill.

Venus (*Anael*) - Pale and Medium Green candle for matters of fertility, health, prosperity and, sensuality. Also wealth (especially with Jupiter). Pink candle for matters of love and friendship. Also sexuality (especially with Mars).

Mars (*Zamael*) - Bright or Deep Red candle for matters of anger, war, protection, revenge, and sexual passion.

Jupiter (*Sachiel*) - Purple or Royal Blue candle for matters of increase, good luck, prosperity, authority, government and justice.

Saturn (*Cassiel*) - Dark Blue/Indigo, Dark Green or black candles for matters of limitation, conclusion, old age, slowing down, longevity, fate, decrease, finding lost or hidden things.

The Outer Planets

Uranus (*Uriel*) - Electric Blue candle for matters of revolution, change, clubs, teams and groups.

Neptune (*Asariel*) - Aqua or Marine-colored candle for matters of illusions, psychic powers, the sea, formlessness, sexual dysfunction, addictions, bad habits, self sacrifice.

Pluto (*Azrael*) - Dark Red, Grey or Black candle for matters of sex, death, secrets, occult powers.

Astrological Signs

Aries people are represented with Bright or Deep Red candles.

Taurus people are represented with Pale or Medium Green candles. (Brown is also a traditional color for Taurus.)

Gemini people are represented with Pale Yellow candles.

Cancer people are represented with White, Pale Blue or Silver candles.

Leo people are represented with Orange, Gold or Red candles.

Virgo people are represented with Golden Yellow or Beige candles.

Libra people are represented with Pink candles

Scorpio people are represented with Dark Red, Grey or Black candles.

Sagittarius people are represented with Purple or Royal Blue candles.

Capricorn people are represented with Indigo or Dark Green candles.

Aquarius people are represented with Electric Blue candles.

Pisces people are represented with Aqua or Marine-colored candles.

Note: Because the colors representing astrological signs are often the same as the colors of the planets that rule them (Aries and Mars, for example), you may wish to make subtle distinctions. For example, you might decide that, in your work, purple will always represent the influence of the planet Jupiter and royal blue will always represent Sagittarius. You might decide that Venus will always be pale green, Taurus medium green and Libra pink. These are the kind of distinctions you may wish to make after determining what types of candles are available to you and most convenient for you. You can then judge what colors are available and what they should represent.

Some Problems and Issues

Bad Planets?

One of the general trends in modern astrology is the tendency to get away from attaching primarily negative associations to certain planets or signs of the zodiac. The Moon, for example, was once said to cause "lunacy" (insanity). Today we think of the Moon as representative of non-rationality rather than irrationality - imagination and mystery rather than madness. Saturn (once called the "Greater Malefic") and Mars (once called the "Lesser Malefic"), specifically, have a long tradition of negative associations. For our purposes, Saturn seems to have been pretty much rehabilitated.

Problems concerning the planet Mars still persist, however. Part of this is perhaps because the angel of Mars is Zamael. Unfortunately, Zamael is sometimes equated with Samael, a fallen angel. Some people may not be comfortable with this. Whether you are or not is up to you. However, from what I understand about the Qabalistic system from which the angelic elements of the planetary systems derive, I do not think that is quite the origin. In Qabalism, as I understand it (and I'm no expert), the Divine Force is supposed to have severe as well as merciful aspects. None of it is supposed to be evil. It is all supposed to simply be part of a balanced understanding of the cosmos. Red - the color of Mars - is also a very traditional and powerful magical color, in use since primordial times. It would be a shame to dispense with it or give it only a minor role.

Of course, the easy answer is simply to do as Ficino originally did - use the planetary influences only and dispense with the associated angelic powers. Although Ficino's reasons for having reservations about angelic magic may not be anything we would share today, those reservations may have some validity. Our planetary system just scratches the surface of angelic magic. When we start dealing with forces on this level, we are entering into the realm of ceremonial magic - an advanced spiritual discipline that requires a lifetime of dedication. Even the very modest angelic system we have here should be handled with caution and reverence. Remember also that many of the angelic elements entered the planetary magic system from Jewish occultism - a tradition where the magician is assumed to be a person of integrity, maturity and wisdom. And whether you use the angelic material or not, keep in mind that the passion, anger and aggression that we associate with Mars have a tremendous destructive potential - and are at the same time part of a healthy personality. The questions about using the Martian influence should perhaps serve as reminders of the importance of properly directing passions and anger. They should also perhaps stand as a warning to use this type of energy sparingly. Martian energy may, in fact, be something that you should avoid using until you are more experienced. Certainly, it should probably not be a primary focus of your work when you are starting out.

This will not seem so limiting when you consider that practically everything that one might use Mars to accomplish can also be accomplished with the energies of the Sun. And any warm color may be considered solar because of the associations of such colors with sunlight at different times of the day. Thus, red candles may be associated with the Sun as well. The solar angel, Michael, is the

Great General of the Hosts of Heaven, so he also has some warrior attributes. Furthermore, Michael's tendency is to support only just causes and fair fights. The energies of Mars, on the other hand, are far less discriminating. Using Solar energies instead of Martian ones helps insure that you are not simply being vindictive or bullying someone. Also, where Zamael tends to be an impulsive and volatile warrior who may not care who suffers the consequences of his rampages, provided they are somehow deserved, Michael is wise and merciful and more willing to be a teacher, to show you where you are going wrong.

Mars and the Sun may, of course, be used together. You might also use Mars, to intensify the effects of the Sun in matters having to do with courage, protection or virility. Indeed, whenever you use Mars, you might want to use the Sun also. Michael, the solar angel, is a conqueror of evil forces. It's a good principle to have in operation whenever Mars is around to make sure that the Martian influences are restricted to their more benevolent and useful aspects.

In general, you might make it standard practice to "soften" the Martian energy with another influence whether that be the Sun or something else. I also find that pine is an herbal scent with Martian associations that generally brings out the more positive, protective aspects of this planetary influence.

Black Candles?

Here is another sticky issue. Should you use black candles? Well first of all, what do black candles represent, really? Basically, black candles represent emptiness. At the beginning, I spoke of the lighting of a candle as representative of creation from nothing. This representation is never stronger than when a black candle is lit. More to the point, black candles are a void, the state of pure potential before something manifests. It is black, as Leo Vinci remarks, within the womb. The earth before it is seeded is also black. As such, black candles may be useful for contemplation and returning the mind to the pure state of formlessness. They are negative, receptive energy, waiting to be filled with something else. By nature, black absorbs rather than radiates, waits for something to vibrate within it rather than producing a vibration of its own. And this can create extra difficulty. Black candles for magical operations must be carefully purified to rid them of any influence they might have absorbed and carefully stored in order to protect them from unwanted influences. This makes them tricky to work with. There are plenty of alter-natives for black candles. For example, various dark or neutral toned candles can be substituted in different operations.

But, should you use black candles? The technical answer is that as long as you have white candles as your primary altar candles, you should be able to use anything you want because you have oriented yourself and your work toward benign intent. The philosophical answer, of course, is that everything depends on your intentions and that the color of candles is irrelevant. The practical answer is that you should never do anything that you do not feel comfortable doing. We have been repeatedly conditioned to think of black candles as representing harmful and negative activity - and, in some candle ritual traditions, they are, in fact, used to represent harmful intent. It may be that this will influence how you view the work you are doing and what events the ritual makes you receptive to. It may set up a destructive resonance. You are dealing with the symbols in your own unconscious mind when you perform a magical operation. What seems wrong to you is wrong for you. Learn to respect your own intuition.

Another possibility might be to follow the tradition that uses black candles to signify bad situations and evil forces which you are trying to banish. This, of course, only reinforces the perhaps unfortunate tradition of portraying black as an "evil" color. An alternative to this would be to use a greenish yellow candle to represent any evil that you wish to banish - especially disease but it can also represent jealousy or malice. (This color, I think, has more to do with auras than it does with planetary energies.) This candle should be a really ugly, poisonous color and should not be reused after the ritual is done. (This tradition seems to apply specifically to banishing evil of non-supernatural origin. If you think you have problems with evil of a supernatural origin, I would urge you not to handle this by yourself. Seek whatever aid your religious tradition advises.)

Exploring Alternatives

The beauty of the system which I have outlined is its flexibility. Please keep in mind that the planetary system I have described does not belong to any specific religious tradition. Ficino limited himself to planetary influences in order to avoid trouble with the Church but that does not mean that his system is specifically Christian. Indeed, he seemed to think that he was working with scientific principles rather than religious mysteries. The angelic powers which were incorporated into later planetary systems, of course, are of Hebraic origin. However, there never seems to have been a sense (at least not in this century) that angelic magic systems were somehow only appropriate for Christians or Jews. Like the planetary systems, the angelic systems seem to be considered universal - appropriate for occultists of all religious backgrounds. However, despite this, people from the Pagan tradition may simply want something with a more distinctly Pagan flavor.

Now, when I say that the system is flexible, I mean that you can leave out some of the correspondences. You don't have to use the angels, if you don't want to - just the colors and the planetary energies they correspond to. Indeed, this was Ficino's original system. We may think it more spiritual to include the angelic elements but in Ficino's day, the truly reverent and pious practice was to leave such powers to the Church and to limit oneself to working with the less exalted planetary influences. It is, therefore, perfectly appropriate to simply use the planetary energies and leave the angelic dimension out.

You can even simplify it beyond that, however. For example, you can just use the colors alone either for visualization or in simple rituals (as some systems do). Even the simplest systems that just use colors, however, without any mention of angels or planets, still often have a color system for astrological signs so that people may be represented in the ritual by candles with colors representing their signs. You may, however, simply choose to use the person's "favorite color" or a color the person commonly wears for the candle representing them.

Can this system be given a more Pagan flavor? As I've said, it's not really necessary, but some people might simply prefer designing rituals that have a consistent flavor with the other ritual work they are doing. One obvious alternative that comes to mind is simply to substitute ancient pagan deities for the angelic powers. The most obvious choice here would the Graeco-Roman deities after whom the planets were named. Apollo (the Sun) Mercury/Hermes, Venus/Aphrodite, Diana/Artemis (the Moon), Mars/Ares, Jupiter/Zeus, Saturn/Kronos, Uranus, Neptune/Poseidon, Pluto/Hades.

There are some real disadvantages here, however. The planetary influences sometimes don't match exactly with the attributes associated with the Graeco-Roman deities. For example, Apollo - in the Classical tradition, at least - doesn't really have the triumphant associations that the Sun does in the planetary system. In Classical myth, he was more a god of the arts and the intellect than of victory and courage.

You may want to find a way to work with variations like this. However, the real problem here is that, even though the planets take the name of Roman gods, the system I have outlined is actually based on Renaissance astrological principles rather than on ancient Classical beliefs. Perhaps you and the deities of Greece and Rome would all be better served if you did research and developed your own system, with its own color correspondences for the candles, that better related to authentic Greek or Roman traditions? Of course, the Renaissance seems to have liked to personify the planetary influences by equating them with the Graeco-Roman deities. If Botticelli's *Venus* really is an attempt to manifest the planetary influence, the artist did this by giving the figure personifying the planet Venus the attributes of the Classical goddess. Just keep in mind that, if you do this, it's a Renaissance classical-revival tradition you are following, not the authentic religion of Greece or Rome.

And what about other pantheons? Celtic, Norse and Egyptian deities are very popular with modern Pagans. And there are all sorts of tables that claim to show you how the gods from those pantheons correspond with the gods of the Graeco-Roman pantheon. It is very tempting to use these correspondences with our planetary system - to make Mercury, for example, into Odin or Tehuti. Personally, I've never been terribly satisfied with that kind of material. I find that these neat systems of correspondence often break down.

Furthermore, the religions associated with these pantheons are not all the same - the Norse and the Egyptians, for example, may have approached their deities very differently. Plugging Graeco-Roman deities into a planetary system makes some sense because those names are used in astrology. However, treating names from other pantheons as interchangeable with Graeco-Roman ones (as if everyone is really worshiping the same deities with different names) can get somewhat forced.

If you are a modern Pagan who takes pride in claiming that your practices somehow reflect the authentic character of an ancient pagan religion, my basic conclusion is to discourage simply substituting pagan deities for the angelic powers. What you should probably do instead is research the ritual practices and magical ethics of a specific authentic tradition. What, for example, would different colors mean in that tradition? Did they have rituals involving light or fire?

Putting the planetary correspondences completely aside, it occurs to me that candles can be used as inexpensive substitutes or supplements for statues that may be traditionally used in rituals from various traditions. They might also be used as apartment sized substitutes for the ritual bonfires some traditions use - the Celtic religion is especially well known for this. Such a ritual fire could get scaled down to involve a single candle. There are numerous possibilities.

If, however, you prefer a more eclectic approach to your practices and frequently mix elements from different traditions and find that this works, then perhaps substitutions would work well for you. Another, more fruitful possibility for Pagans who do not like the Hebraic character of this system might be to study the Ishtar myth and create eclectic rituals that work with the metaphor of the planets as the seven veils of the Goddess. So you might draw aside Her pink veil for guidance in love, Her yellow veil for help with communication, Her orange veil for courage and vitality, etc. If I recall the myth correctly, Ishtar sheds her veils in order to gain entrance to the Underworld. The Underworld, of course, is often taken as a symbol of the Unconscious Mind (the place where mystical symbols are born) and this, it seems to me, could be a rewarding avenue to explore.

There is also good news for those who are interested in Norse traditions. However, the system I would suggest is very different from the planetary one outlined above. One thing about candles is that they can be easily marked. Letters or symbols can be very easily cut into the wax with a warm knife. Those interested in Norse traditions might experiment with marking candles with runes, rune rows or bindrunes to aid with their rituals. Some Norse systems do use color correspondences and you can experiment with some of those when selecting candle colors. Or you might simply use the earth tones - greens, browns - associated with the natural materials that seem preferred for rune staves and not worry about color correspondences.

I will talk a little bit more about carving symbols in candles later. This will work well with any system that uses a magical alphabet and that opens some intriguing possibilities, as we'll see.

The really good news, however, is that the planetary system doesn't really need to be modified at all. It makes use of the archetypical principles of Western astrology which do not belong to any particular magical or religious tradition.

Incense and Oils

Incenses and oils are included in candle rituals in most of the sources I have reviewed for this manual. Incense contributes a great deal to the creation of a spiritual atmosphere and has been used for that purpose since ancient times. Oils are used to dress candles, to charge them for a particular ritual purpose and to help in the process of dedicating them to a particular planetary influence. I'll talk a little more about the specifics of this kind of operation when I talk about ritual design.

There are several different kinds of traditional ritual incense available in metaphysical stores. Generally, these are in resin form and do not light well by themselves. What you have to do is buy charcoal (also usually sold where the incense is available) and light it in the incense burner and dump the incense on top. This burns the incense and allows it to give off its scented smoke. Frankincense is a popular incense of this type but myrrh, copal and other varieties are also available.

Of course, you can also get cake incense in most or all of these traditional scents. This is also burned in a incense burner. It is probably the most familiar type of incense and is usually shaped into cones. It requires no charcoal. You simply light the tip of the cone and let the incense burn down. You can also get incense on sticks - a slim stick is coated with the incense but one end is left bare so that you can hold the incense. You light the tip. Stick incense is very popular (there may now even be more varieties easily available to you than cake incense) and very useful - especially if you are creating rituals where the incense is to be carried around as part of the ritual as if often done to sanctify a sacred space for magical work.

A traditional incense burner, used with both resin and cake incense, is a metal bowl or plate with a bell shaped lid with holes in it. When working with charcoal, putting the lid on tends to extinguish the incense. You may also find this to be true with some varieties of cake incense. If you find that it goes out, just relight it and continue with the lid off. Sometimes incense burners of this type are set up to be suspended from chains. If you are using resins and charcoal, the dish should be large enough to hold the charcoal and a small heap of incense. If you are using cake incense, it can be smaller but make sure that the size of cake fits in the closed bowl.

People from Pagan and Wiccan traditions may like to use a small iron cauldron to hold incense. However, some Wiccan traditions teach that the cauldron and the incense burner are two different things and that the cauldron should be left free for other purposes.

If you are using stick incense, you can get all sorts of incense holders with little holes in them where you can place the incense so you don't have to keep it in your hand all the time. As I've said, this is a good type of incense to use if you carry the incense around at all.

You can also get very elaborate incense burners, designed for use in church processions, which are hung on the end of a chain so that they can be carried. These, however, are complicated gizmos. (Don't try swinging or twirling the thing the way the altar server does. It takes a lot of practice - and a lot of room.) Another possibility would be to place the incense burner or cauldron on a sturdy, heat resistant tray in order to make it easy to carry. Incense burners get quite hot so be careful of touching them! Also be careful not to place them directly on surfaces that easily burn or melt. (Generations of occult practitioners have learned this the hard way!) This is another advantage of stick incense: the burning part is away from the surface you are working on. The sticks do tend to drop ash and that's messy, but it doesn't do permanent damage.

Whatever type you decide to use, frankincense is a very traditional multi-purpose ritual incense. Or you may prefer to burn an incense associated with a planetary influence that is important in your ritual.

Varieties of Incense and Oils

As I have said, I have been unable to determine whether or not burning colored candles was a normal practice in Renaissance planetary magic traditions. They did, however, gather herbs and flowers associated with the planetary influence they were trying to strengthen. You can often find ready made oils and incense oriented toward specific planetary influences. The disadvantage here is that you have no way of knowing exactly what is in these preparations. You can't even begin to tell whether or not they are formulated correctly without some knowledge of what should be in them. Also, they may not be available in all areas of the country. I am, therefore, including here a very brief and by no means exhaustive guide to herbs and flowers associated with each of the seven planetary influences known in ancient times. These scented materials can be used both in oils for dressing the candles and in incense for use in the ritual. With few exceptions, I have selected only the materials which I felt would probably be easiest to obtain in oil or incense form.

Occasionally there are different traditional associations for the same plants or something else also makes sense. Where this happens, I have noted it.

Sun

(Often associated with plants that somehow resemble it shape or color - large, round, red, orange or yellow fruit or flowers. Medicinal herbs associated with the heart.)

Bay (an especially strong association)

Benzoin (sometimes associated with Venus)

Chamomile

Carnation

Chrysanthemum

Cinnamon (sometimes associated with Jupiter)

Copal

Frankincense (A very traditional scent that is sometimes also associated with Saturn, but customarily placed here.)

Lime

Marigold

Orange

Peony

Pineapple

Rosemary

Sandalwood

Sunflower

Moon

(Once again also associated with things that resemble it in size, shape or color - pale flowers, crescent shaped flowers or fruit or large, round flowers or fruit. It is also associated with plants that grow near water or that have a high water content.)

Aloe

Camellia

Coconut

Eucalyptus

Gardenia

Grape

Jasmine

Lemon (Mercury also seems to like lemon scented things.)

Lily

Lotus

Myrrh (A very traditional scent that is also very strongly associated with Saturn.)

Myrtle (also associated with Venus)

Wintergreen

Mercury

(Often associated with "airy" plants - that is plants with small, feathery leaves. Plants with medicinal associations with the nerves.)

Almond

Bergamot

Dill

Fennel

Lavender

Lemon grass

Lemon Verbena

Lily of the Valley

Mace

Marjoram

Parsley

Venus
(Often associated with, pretty, fragrant flowers or plants with red fruit or pink or red blossoms.)

Apple

Banana (also associated with the Moon because of its crescent shape)

Cardamon

Cherry

Licorice

Lilac

Raspberry

Rose

Spearmint

Strawberry

Thyme

Vanilla

Violet

Mars
(Often associated with prickly plants, spicy-tasting plants or plants with a sharp or acrid scent.)

Allspice

Basil

Chili Pepper

Coriander

Cumin

Dragon's Blood

Garlic

Ginger

High John the Conqueror

Mustard

Onion

Pennyroyal

Peppermint

Pine (Pine oil seems to work especially well with Mars. It really brings out the vital and protective aspects of the Martian influence.)

Tobacco

Wormwood

Jupiter
(Often associated with plants with a pleasant, warm odor and medicinal plants associated with the liver or circulatory system.)

Anise

Clove

Honeysuckle

Hyssop

Nutmeg

Sage (Traditionally placed here because of its medicinal assoc-iation with the liver. Because of its association with wisdom and longevity, I feel it might also be associated with Saturn.)

Saturn

(Often associated with poisonous and narcotic plants, trees that have rings, as the planet does, and plants with cooling qualities like barley. Most of these aren't terribly aromatic. Some of the more traditional ritual incense varieties, especially Myrrh also sometimes get associated with Saturn.)

Barley	Patchouli (probably the most promising choice)
Comfrey	
Cypress	Opium Poppy (also associated with the Moon)
Hemp	
Lobelia	Quince
Mimosa	Spikenard (sometimes associated with Venus)
Mullein	
Pansy	Tamarind
	Yew

Please note: some books on herbalism will give you recipes for concoctions to eat or drink - teas, etc. You may wish to add these elements to your rituals or ritual preparations. However, be very careful because many of these references are, unfortunately, not as careful as they should be about advising readers of the toxicity of some herbal ingredients or the potential for allergic reactions.

Other Traditional Incenses and Oils:

I should also mention that there are quite a few traditional occult incenses and oils available. They have names like "Voodoo", "Come to Me", "Fast Luck", "Exodus", "Commanding", and "Black Cat". Some are named after saints or deities. There are hundreds of them, all intended for different purposes - some benign and some aggressive. It's folk magic pure and simple - what a southern friend of mine calls "granny magic" after the wise women of the southern United States. Such traditions mix Christian elements with folk traditions stretching back to ancient European paganism as well as native elements and seemingly original elements. I'm not going to discuss these oils and incenses in detail here. (In many cases, there doesn't really seem to be any set formula for these concoctions.) But if this interests you, go ahead and try it out.

Marking Candles

As I said, when discussing runes, it is easy to carve things into candles. Among the things that might be helpful in these rituals are first of all the planetary symbols, which will designate a specific candle as representing a specific planetary influence.

Sun -	☉	Jupiter -	♃
Moon -	☽	Saturn -	♄
Mercury -	☿	Uranus -	♅
Venus -	♀	Neptune -	♆
Mars -	♂	Pluto -	♇

If you are using a candle selected in order to correspond with some-one's astrological sun sign, you might want to carve the symbol for that sign on the candle.

Aries -	♈	Leo -	♌	Sagittarius -	♐
Taurus -	♉	Virgo -	♍	Capricorn -	♑
Gemini -	♊	Libra -	♎	Aquarius -	♒
Cancer -	♋	Scorpio -	♏	Pisces -	♓

Working with Tarot Cards

The runes, of course, are a magical alphabet. Carving symbols in the candles will work for any system that uses a magical alphabet. This opens many intriguing possibilities. For example, the cards in the Major Arcana of a Tarot deck traditionally correspond with the letters of the Hebrew alphabet. The Major Arcana cards also have assoc-iation with various astrological concepts. You could set up quite an intricate series of correspondences between the cards and candles. This creates interesting possibilities for more developed magical procedures using candles and Tarot cards. Ficino's practices also seem to have included meditation upon pictures embodying the characteristics of the planetary influences. (You will recall that Botticelli's *Venus* may have been created for a similar purpose.) He seems to have been somewhat ambivalent about this practice because of a traditional Medieval condemnation of creating amulets by drawing planetary influences into images or jewelry and "storing" them there for later use. (It was, however, arguably permissible to make use of the planets' "natural" influence on herbs and minerals - especially for medicinal purposes.)

We are getting into more advanced material here, however. You may want to master the other concepts in this text before trying to relate them to the often complex world of the Tarot. It also helps if you are already a Tarot reader or familiar with that discipline. If you like simple rituals rather than intricate systems, integrating the Tarot into candle rituals may not even be for you. Gareth Knight has said that "...the occult falls between religion and science. It is, in fact, a great rubbish heap of discarded fragments of unwanted religion and science. Some of these fragments, perhaps most, have been discarded for good reason. However some have been thrown there simply because at some time they went out of fashion and subsequent generations have passed them by...." Occultism is an exercise in hunting for forgotten treasures. Now, rather than a "rubbish heap", I like to think of occultism more as an attic where many wonderful things have been stored over time and forgotten. This is probably especially true of the Tarot.

Despite legends to the contrary, Tarot cards first appeared in the late Middle Ages and Renaissance. In her book, *The Mystical Tarot*, occult historian Rosemary Ellen Guiley records that they seem to be a combination of two different kinds of cards. The first were decks of playing cards, very like our modern ones, numbered and divided into suits. The other were cards - intended, perhaps, for educational purposes - depicting different moral or spiritual concepts. To this day, the Tarot is divided into two parts: the Major Arcana, a set of mystical picture cards and the Minor Arcana, more similar to playing cards, still divided into suits and numbered. At some point fortune-telling got added to the "games" played with the cards. Attaching occult significance to numbers is a very old practice and this may have influenced the tradition of practicing divination with playing cards.

By the eighteenth century, the fifteenth century French Marseilles deck had become the standard Tarot deck. Some occultists began attempting to relate the Tarot to ancient Egyptian mystical concepts. Mostly, this was wishful thinking. (This was well before archae-ologists determined what ancient Egyptians actually believed.) But association of the mysterious Tarot with ancient Egypt still persists. Later, especially in the nineteenth century, the cards were linked to astrology and the Qabala and, with the Qabala, to the Hebrew alphabet. (I should note that Jewish scholars are often very disturbed by the misconceptions that non-Jewish occultists have about the Qabala and by what they perceive as a distorted understanding of this mystical system.) Many important occultists worked with the Tarot, changing the numbering of the cards and making other alterations. What seems to have happened was not that forgotten, ancient concepts were discovered hidden in the cards but that new, sophisticated meanings were given to the cards. These new meanings, in turn, influenced the symbolic elements that appeared in new versions of the Tarot. The cards became a repository of many layers of esoteric thought.

The occult thinker associated most strongly with the modern development of the Tarot is Arthur Edward Waite (1857-1942). A member of the turn-of-the-century occult society, the Golden Dawn, he saw universal symbolic meanings in the cards of the Marseilles deck. He redesigned them, enhancing the symbolism of the Major Arcana and giving the Minor Arcana cards evocative pictures as well. However, Waite did not like speculation that the Tarot, although mystically symbolic, was derived from other occult systems - the Qabala, for example. He wrote, in his *Pictorial Key to the Tarot*, that the "true Tarot is symbolism; it speaks no other language...[I]t is a presentation of universal ideas by means of universal types." In general, however, the Golden Dawn did develop such advanced Qabalistic associations for the cards. (And, it produced its own Tarot deck.) A later Golden Dawn occultist - Paul Foster Case (1884-1954) - devised a system using a Waite influenced deck that codified correspondences with the Qabala, astrology, and Hebrew letters. To me, this kind of development of Tarot material seems legitimate. These systems are helpful in organizing the raw material of Tarot symbolism and certainly have influenced the later development of Tarot mysticism.

Today, Waite's deck, the Rider-Waite deck (published in 1910, the art work done by Golden Dawn psychic Pamela Colman Smith) is the most familiar Tarot deck. It has influenced many others. This is the deck I will refer to here. The next best known is the one designed by the very important ceremonial magician, Aleister Crowley (1875-1947), who had also spent time in the Golden Dawn. Crowley developed sophisticated Qabalistic and astrological associations for the cards. Generally, the Tarot has become a multi-layered system of mystical images - no longer used simply for fortunetelling but also for contemplation of very advanced concepts.

Still, Tarot cards are most commonly used for divinatory purposes. As I mentioned earlier, both Ficino and especially Pico were skeptical about the use of astrology for divination - predicting the future or finding lost objects. Aside from their Christian belief in free will, both Ficino and Pico were strongly influenced by the Greek philosopher, Plato. One of Plato's basic teachings was that the spiritual dimension was more powerful than the material dimension. The idea that the human will - a spiritual force - was subordinate to the influence of a natural phenomenon like the influence of the planets went against this principle. I tend to interpret the planetary magic of these Renaissance traditions as an attempt to assert the control of the human will over the influence of the planets, making the material realm subordinate to the spiritual realm, as Plato said it should be.

Taking a divinatory tool like a Tarot card and using it to magically change reality rather than simply submitting to its predictions about reality, is in keeping with this idea. This does not mean that you should not heed the wisdom revealed in Tarot divinations. (Indeed, it's a good practice to seek the advice of the cards before attempting magical operations.) However, you should keep in mind that you can use these images to assert your will as well as to inform it.

A good book that might be helpful for this purpose is *Tarot Spells* by Janina Renee. Renee's approach seems to basically take card combinations that would generally be read as predicting certain things and use those combinations as visualization tools to influence events. Her techniques are easily adapted for use in rituals using candles to represent and heighten the influences associated with the cards. Indeed, she associates colors with magical effects and recommends the use of colored candles in ritual operations. However, her method doesn't relate to astrological principles but only to the divinatory meanings generally associated with the cards.

Here's a list of the cards of the Major Arcana, their basic meaning and their astrological correspondences. (Each card corresponds with either a planet, a sign of the zodiac or one of the mystical elements.) Planetary correspondences are **bold faced**. I will also give the Hebrew letter associated with each card, so that you know what symbol to carve on the candle (or you might use the card's number, perhaps in Roman numerals as they appear on the cards). This is complicated, but it will be simpler if, at first, you focus only on the astrological correspondences with planets. Please keep in mind that, as always, systems differ. (The one below is based on Paul Foster Case's system.) If you find something that you prefer or that makes better sense to you, don't hesitate to use it.

0. The Fool	Air	Aleph	א
Beginnings, innocence, lack of experience.			
1. **The Magician**	**Mercury**	**Beth**	ב
Effectiveness, skill, intellect, creative power, will.			
2. **The High Priestess**	**the Moon**	**Gimel**	ג
Mystery, hidden influences, mystical matters.			
3. **The Empress**	**Venus**	**Daleth**	ד
Abundance, fertility, sensuality, prosperity, luxury.			

4. The Emperor — Aries — Heh — ה
   Authority, leadership.

5. The Hierophant — Taurus — Vau — ו
   Institutions, obedience to tradition, the conventional.

6. The Lovers — Gemini — Zain — ז
   Choices, forces to be brought into harmony.

7. The Chariot — Cancer — Cheth — ח
   Victory, mastery of emotions.

8. Strength — Leo — Teth — ט
   Courage, spiritual fortitude.

9. The Hermit — Virgo — Yod — י
   Study, wisdom, a learning experience.

10. **The Wheel of Fortune** — **Jupiter** — **Kaph** — כ
    Good fortune, surprises, change.

11. Justice — Libra — Lamed — ל
    Justice, legal matters, balance.

12. The Hanged Man — Water — Mem — מ
    Stagnation, suspension, mystical contemplation.

13. Death — Scorpio — Nun — נ
    Transformation, radical change, renewal.

14. Temperance — Sagittarius — Samekh — ס
    Moderation, adaptation.

15. The Devil — Capricorn — Ayin — ע
    Greed, materialism, wrong priorities.

16. **The Tower** — **Mars** — **Peh** — פ
    Violence, destruction, ruined ambition.

17. The Star — Aquarius — Tzaddi — צ
    Inspiration, communication, hope, health.

18. The Moon — Pisces — Qoph — ק
    Dreams, imagination, illusions, hidden danger.

19. **The Sun** — **the Sun** — **Resh** — ר
    Joy, freedom, achievement, vitality.

20. Judgment — Fire — Shin — ש
    Awakening, understanding, assessment.

21. **The World** — **Saturn** — **Tau** — ת
    Conclusion, culmination, destiny, success.

You see how complex it is. There are many layers of meaning. The cards associated with the mystical elements and the signs of the zodiac can be especially confusing. What does Fire have to do with Judgment? The meanings of the cards often relate well to the zodiac signs but seem to have peculiar associations with the planet ruling the sign. Sure, Taurus is known to be conservative and Libra is known to be just but what do the attributes of these cards have to with Venus, the planet that rules those signs? Neither of these cards would make good, alternate Venus cards. Notice also that the Moon card does not correspond astrologically with the Moon (that's the High Priestess) or even with the Moon ruled sign of Cancer. The card does indeed embody Lunar qualities, but it is associated with the sign of Pisces, ruled by Jupiter and (this makes sense) Neptune. The card associated with Cancer is the Chariot, a victory card that doesn't clearly relate to the aspects usually associated with that sign or with its ruler, the Moon. Because of things like this, in the beginning, at least, I would stress the astrological associations of cards corresponding with planets instead of those associated with signs of the zodiac. As you study more, much of the rest will make more sense.

Fortunately, most of the planetary correspondences **do** make good sense - Venus and the Empress, for example, or the Wheel of Fortune and Jupiter. There are, however, a few problems. For example, we don't find the protective aspects of the Sun in the Tarot card that corresponds to it. The Magician doesn't really capture the aspects of Mercury that deal with speed, youth or communication. The Tower has none of Mars' heroic aspects - it merely emphasizes its destructiveness. It takes some thought to see how The World's associations with conclusion and destiny match up with Saturn's association with boundaries and limitation.

Still, because of these changes in emphasis, the cards often provide new insights into astrological concepts. The planet Saturn, for example, was long considered a negative influence and even called the "Great Malefic", a joyless energy ruling scarcity and decline. Studying the Tarot reveals more positive aspects. Representing Mercury with the Magician gives Mercury associations with "making things happen" that it doesn't always have even though it is usually thought of as making things happen **faster**. *Also, for ritual purposes* *you can expand the associations of a card somewhat to better cover the planetary influence it represents.*

Selecting Cards for Rituals - My advice is to use only what make sense to you. Don't force confusing astrological associations. When creating candle rituals with Tarot cards, I suggest, in fact, that you ignore some of the astrological associations of the cards. (Remember, focus on the astrological associations only of the cards that represent planets and not those that correspond with astrological signs.) *Choose one or two cards for their planetary associations. Use other cards the way Renee uses them - let their divinatory meanings help you focus on the desired outcome for the ritual and ignore the astrological connections.* (If you want to adapt Renee's rituals for use with our system, simply identify what planetary influence is most closely associated with the desired effect of the ritual and add the card associated with that planet to the ritual if it is not already there. Use candles, oils, incense and spoken material related to that dominant planetary influence.) I will go into more detail about ritual design later.

Cards to Represent People - Keep in mind that when working with Tarot cards, the cards associated with astrological signs don't usually represent people born under those signs. People are generally represented with the court cards of the Minor Arcana. Kings are mature men. Queens are women. Knights are young, active men. Pages are teenage girls and children of either sex. The different suits of the Minor Arcana - Wands, Cups, Swords and Pentacles in Rider-Waite - correspond with people's coloring. (The system is biased toward Northern European Caucasians. Most of the rest of the world ends up being Pentacles! There are ways of modifying this system to better reflect the whole human family. If you are going to read the cards, such modifications may be important).

There is an alternative better suited to our type of ritual, however. The four suites of the Minor Arcana represent the four mystical elements. Pentacles are Earth and Cups are Water. In the Rider-Waite system, the images seem to have been created with the assumption that Wands are Fire and Swords are Air. (Although other systems switch them around and it does make some sense in terms of occult tradition: Raphael, the Angel of Air, traditionally holds a Wand. Michael, the Angel of Fire, traditionally holds a Sword.)

What this means in terms of using cards to signify people is that you could choose a court card from the suit of Wands to represent any person born under the astrological signs of Aries, Leo or Sagittarius (the Fire signs). Cards from the suit of Cups would represent people born under the Water signs of Cancer, Scorpio or Pisces. Similarly a Sword representing Air could be used for a Gemini, Libra or Aquarius person. A Pentacle card would represent a person born under an Earth sign: Taurus, Virgo or Capricorn. (There are more advanced and specific associations of Minor Arcana cards with astrological signs but this simpler method will work for our purposes.) This would probably make sense if you were also going to represent the person with a candle associated with his or her astrological sign.

Adding the Rest of the Minor Arcana Cards - Minor Arcana cards also have divinatory meanings and can be used to help focus these rituals. They tend to represent specific mundane events while Major Arcana cards relate more to mystical or ethical concepts. If you are using them in a ritual for any purpose other than representing a person's astrological sign, I would ignore the astrological association and concentrate only on the divinatory meaning.

The four suits of the Minor Arcana have general divinatory meanings and the specific cards develop those themes. Wands represent vitality and enterprise. Cups represent love, spirituality and emotion. Swords represent conflict, victory and defeat. Pentacles represent wealth, fertility and practical skill. Aces are pure energy and are good cards to give an extra "push" with the appropriate energy, especially to get something started. Generally, they have positive interpretations. Twos signify balance and partnership. Threes symbolize increase and development. Fours have to do with stability and matters coming to rest. Fives tend to be negative and deal with instability. Sixes tend to be positive and deal with accomplishment or mastery of a situation. Sevens signify spiritual challenges. Eights, nines and tens tend to represent various forms of abundance or even excess. Specifically, eights often involve setting priorities. Nines have to do with the culmination of a cycle. Tens somehow herald a new beginning. They represent a suit's energy spilling over into a new phase or, at least, a need for renewal of that suit's energy. Pages represent messages. Knights represent speed and rapidly unfolding events.   Queens represent awareness.   Kings represent worldly success and control - a powerful person coming to your aid. I should point out that placing a card of either the Major or Minor Arcana upside down traditionally changes its meaning - diminishing it, reversing it, or twisting it.

Some important positive cards would be the Two of Cups (love and friendship); the Three of Cups (harmony); the Three of Wands (success), the Four of Wands (prosperity); the Six of Wands (victory); the Six of Swords (a better future); the Six of Pentacles (charity); the Seven of Wands (courage); the Eight of Wands (speed); the Eight of Pentacles (professional skill), the Nine of Cups (material happiness), the Ten of Cups (a happy life, family bliss) the Ten of Pentacles (wealth, inheritance). Some cards with negative associations are the Two of Swords (stasis and indecision); the Five of Wands (strife); the Five of Swords (deception); Five of Cups (regret, disappointment); the Five of Pentacles (destitution); the Seven of Cups (illusions); the Eight of Swords (restrictions), the Nine of Swords (sorrow); the Ten of Swords (defeat and destruction).

You should have more use for the positive cards than the negative ones. You might use the negative cards to represent something that you are trying to banish, however. You might also use cards that suggest stasis or inactivity to restrict the actions of an enemy. If you read the Tarot and find a negative card in a reading, you might set up a ritual to protect the person for whom the reading was done against that influence. I'll discuss this more in the section on ritual design.

RITUAL DESIGN

Timing Rituals

The Wheel of the Year

Modern Pagans use a calendar of festivals derived from the traditions of the ancient Celts. The holy day which probably has greatest significance for people practicing candle rituals would be Imbolc, also called Brigantia. Vinci identifies this as the ancient feast of the Celtic goddess, Brigid, daughter of the god Dagda. He reports that it was later Christianized and became known as the feast of Candlemas (which, since we are dealing with candle rituals, is what we will call it here). It traditionally falls on February 2. The feast has great connections to light and fire and also with purification. There is a tradition of lighting every lamp in the house on this festival. Furthermore, the custom in Christian churches was to designate this day as the day on which all the candles to be used for the next year would be consecrated. Every practitioner of candle magic should probably find some way of marking this day if it is in any way connected with his or her religious tradition.

One practical problem in candle burning is what to do with the used candles after the ritual. I was originally taught that they could not be reused and that, in fact, they should be reverently buried in the earth! I could see that this could potentially cause quite an environmental problem - at least in my own backyard. I liked the ritual significance of giving the used candles "funerals" but it simply wasn't practical. What was called for was another ritual. So how might one ritualize the disposal of used candles? Perhaps one could set aside a special day when old ritual candles are discarded? Candlemas seems to be a logical choice. On Candlemas you might purchase and perform a blessing ritual on new candles - a selection of all colors and types likely to be used for the coming year. (Of course, you could still buy more new candles as needed throughout the year!) Part of the custom of lighting every light in the house could be to light all your old candles, one last time, while the blessing ritual is going on. You would not have to burn them down all the way. After the ritual is completed, you could reverently dispose of any old candles. You might wrap them in paper and discard them in the trash or - since candle making is not a difficult craft - melt them down and make new candles, perhaps for non-ritual use.

Or you could come up with a way of ritualizing the practice of reusing old candles in a way consistent with the Pagan "wheel of the year" calender of festivals. This cycle follows the agricultural year, marking the lengthening and shortening of the days and, with it, autumn harvests, winter fallow and the regeneration of spring. The Pagan calendar can be used to reawaken awareness of the cycles of nature which so dominated the lives of our ancestors. You might try ritually cleansing and reverently storing the used candles from your rituals. You would then dedicate a specific part of the year to using up these candles. For example, you might, as much as possible, use only used candles in ritual between Samhain (Halloween, October 31) and Candlemas (February 2). New candles would only be used if you had no used candle of the appropriate color or type. Since Samhain is the ancient holiday marking the close of the harvest, it would make sense to rely on stored things rather than fresh things in the period after Samhain - just as our ancestors had to live on stored food in the winter. Any used candles left over at Candlemas would be disposed of in the reverent manner I described earlier. (If you find that this doesn't make a dent in your supply of used candles, you might extend your customary "used candle" season to the feast of Beltane on May 1. You would still bless a supply of new candles on Candlemas but not start using them until Beltane.)

A simple ritual which I must confess I have never tried but which I must share is called "Drawing Down the Sun". Charmaine Dey records this practice in her book *The Magic Candle*. It sounds like a good way to light your sanctuary candle. In theory, the sanctuary candle is a sort of "perpetual flame". (You don't actually leave it burning all the time for safety reasons but when it is replaced, the new candle is lit from the flame of the old candle.) Once a year, you can "recharge" the power of your sanctuary candles by lighting one directly from the Sun itself. This is done out doors in a place where it will not create a fire hazard - perhaps in a backyard grill. You light a piece of charcoal by directing the light of the Sun with a magnifying glass. You ignite wood chips or paper from the charcoal. (You might practice doing this a few times before the ceremony. Dey suggests using saltpeter as an accelerant for the wood chips. Be careful with flammable chemicals!) You then light the new candle with flame taken from the fire kindled in this manner. Dey records that the customary time to do this is Holy Thursday - the Thursday before Easter - or on the Vernal Equinox (March 21). For our practices, it might be a good thing to do on Candlemas, if the winter sun is strong enough and the weather is favorable. (Beltane also sounds like a promising festival for this activity - especially if you pick that day to mark the end of your "used candle" season.)

Working with the Moon

It is traditional to time magical operations to coincide with the appropriate phases of the moon. Calendars showing the phases of the moon are fairly easy to get. Moon phases are also often included on the weather pages in many newspapers.

Here are the basics: It is considered a bad practice to perform rituals or to begin a series of rituals on the first day of the New Moon - when the moon is said to be "dark". Long tradition says that all projects (mundane as well as magical) begun on that day will fail. The moon's power is said to be strongest, of course when the moon is full. This is a good time to perform rituals. It is good to begin a series of rituals (called a "Novena" in our system) or any project when the moon is waxing (increasing in size). Begin a day or so after the New Moon (but not on the New Moon itself) and work up through the Full Moon. Rituals intended to banish something from your life or to cause something to dwindle or lose power are said to be more effective when the moon is waning (decreasing in size). In that case, you begin with the Full Moon and end right before the moon goes dark, sending whatever it is away "with this moon."

Astrological Systems

The system we are using is based on astrological principles. A relevant question, of course, is whether further knowledge of astrology is necessary in order to use this system. At the risk of sounding glib, I will point out that the things which it is actually necessary to know in this life are very few. Why, many people get by very well without knowing a single thing about candle magic - imagine that! However, more knowledge is always a helpful thing to aspire to. And, in practice, the planetary influences will make more sense to you if you understand basic astrological symbolism and principles - how the different signs of the zodiac relate to the four mystical elements of Earth, Air, Fire and Water, for example. It is also extremely helpful to understand enough about astrology to look up and understand which planets are favorably aspected and which planets are in favorable aspect to each other at the time when you want to do your ritual work. This will help you select which planetary influences you will have the most success with and which ones you can use most easily with each other. Good, basic books about astrology come and go. You should have no difficulty finding one. Make sure, however, that it discusses planets in aspect (or in transit) to each other and that it stresses traditional concepts rather than new innovations.

The Days of the Week

When we think of astrology, of course, we think primarily of how the year is divided up between the various signs of the zodiac and the planetary energies which rule the signs. What many people don't understand is that planetary energies also rule both the days of the week and the hours of the day.

Our English days of the week are called after gods from the Norse pantheon - Tyr (Tuesday), Woden (Wednesday), Thor (Thursday), Freya (Friday) - except, interestingly enough, Saturday. Saturday follows instead the pattern of southern Europe where the names of Graeco-Roman deities are used. (And if you speak French, Italian or Spanish you might take a moment to find the Latin deity names in the days of the week in those languages.) Northern Europe seems to have used the names of the Norse gods who correspond most closely to the deities used in the south. But the days do not seem to be named so much after deities as after astrological principles - the Sun and the Moon are included in both the southern and northern lists and all the deities have corresponding planets in the ancient seven planet system.

Here is what you end up having: the Sun (Sunday), the Moon (Monday), Mars (Tuesday), Mercury (Wednesday), Jupiter (Thursday), Venus (Friday) and Saturn (Saturday). Basically, you have a day of the week for every planetary energy.

Now we can stop right here, if you like, because what I've just given you is a system for determining the most appropriate day of the week for working with specific planetary energies. Later, we will talk about compatibilities between energies and from that you can determine alternate days on which to work should the day ruled by the planet you wish to work with not be convenient.

The Planetary Hours

However, there is also a system for dividing up each day so that each of its twenty-four hours has its own planetary energy. Even if you are simply going to be working with days of the week, it's good to know this system so you can at least determine what times of day might be bad for working with certain planetary influences.

There are two ways of working with this system. You can start at sunrise - probably the more ancient way of doing it and in many ways very elegant, but cumbersome to learn and work with. Or you can simply start the day at midnight as our modern clocks do. Starting at midnight is the simpler system and it is the one that I will use here. (Later, when you become more advanced, you may want to change, but this system is easier to learn.)

There are some rules for this system. First, you have to be reasonably punctual about following it. Once you have designated which system you are going to use, you have to operate within its parameters. (That's right - even though by deciding to work from midnight instead of from sunrise, you have decided at which hour the various planetary hours will fall, once you have selected the system you are going to use, you must follow it consistently. Even when there are several alternative forms, ritual acts seem to take on a great deal of power by having many people all doing the same thing down through the years and investing belief in the effectiveness of that ritual custom. Even though I try to give you room to be creative, at the same time, I wouldn't want to miss out on this potential power source by being sloppy and imprecise.) For example, if you are going to work within the hour of Jupiter then you must start within the hour of Jupiter. The good news is that you can begin your ritual at any time within the hour of Jupiter and even if the ritual runs longer than the hour of Jupiter, it still belongs to the hour of Jupiter. (The same is true of the other planets.)

Always work in standard time. Ignore the shift to daylight savings time for the purposes of timing your rituals. (You might keep a special clock, always set to standard time, so that you don't forget.)

Now, how do you determine which hour falls when?

Well, you can follow the table on pages 56 & 57. But what if you want to memorize this material? Is there any pattern to it?

In fact, there is a pattern and it's actually pretty simple. The planetary hours follow a specific sequence. The sequence is best understood as starting at midnight on Sunday and repeating over and over again throughout the rest of the week and starting all over again the next Sunday at midnight.

As you can see from the table, each planet rules one hour. There are 24 hours in a day. When you complete the series it starts over and so on to infinity.

The sequence of planetary hours is always: Sun, Venus, Mercury, Moon, Saturn, Jupiter, Mars. (This and what planet rules what day is all the information you really need to memorize.)

Looking at the table, you will see something very interesting and helpful. This system works out so that each day begins at midnight with the hour of the planet traditionally given rulership of that day! So Sunday begins at midnight with the hour of the Sun, Monday begins at midnight with the hour of the Moon, Tuesday begins at midnight with the hour of Mars, Wednesday with hour of Mercury, etc.

Furthermore, you can see that the hour of the planetary energy ruling each day (the Sun on Sunday, Jupiter on Thursday, Venus on Friday etc.) repeats each day at 7:00 am, at 2:00 pm and at 9:00 pm.

They automatically fall that way with no adjustments on your part. Furthermore, in the system we are using, they all last exactly one hour and begin on the hour. This system assumes an equally-divided, twenty-four hour day. (This, the great advantage of using midnight as the reference point rather than sunrise. The hours don't shift starting times from week to week as the time of sunrise changes as in other systems and the "hours" do not change length to compensate for variations in the length of time between sunrises as the seasons progress.) The sequence is the same for every week of every year into infinity. What could be simpler?

You can actually train yourself to use this system by setting an alarm to go off at Midnight, 7:00 am, 2:00 pm and 9:00 pm. When the alarm goes off you say to yourself, for example, on Wednesdays: "Today is Wednesday. Wednesday is ruled by Mercury. It is now the hour of Mercury. The previous hour was the hour of Venus. The hour after this one will be the hour of the Moon." On Saturday you would say "Today is Saturday, ruled by Saturn. This is the hour of Saturn. The previous hour belonged to the Moon. The one following belongs to Jupiter." And so on for all the days of the week. Pretty soon, you will have the whole sequence memorized and be able to practice counting back and forward for as many hours as you need on any day of the week. When you've mastered that, the next exercise is to look at the clock at random times during the day and see if you can figure out what the planetary hour is at that time and on that particular day of the week.

The fact that the ruler for a particular day has its hour repeated daily at both 7:00 am and 9:00 p.m. means that those who wish to perform daily rituals honoring the planetary influences ruling that day can do so upon rising each morning and before going to bed each night.

	Sunday	Monday	Tuesday	Wednesday	Thursday	Friday	Saturday
Midnight	Sun	Moon	Mars	Mercury	Jupiter	Venus	Saturn
1:00 AM	Venus	Saturn	Sun	Moon	Mars	Mercury	Jupiter
2:00 AM	Mercury	Jupiter	Venus	Saturn	Sun	Moon	Mars
3:00 AM	Moon	Mars	Mercury	Jupiter	Venus	Saturn	Sun
4:00 AM	Saturn	Sun	Moon	Mars	Mercury	Jupiter	Venus
5:00 AM	Jupiter	Venus	Saturn	Sun	Moon	Mars	Mercury
6:00 AM	Mars	Mercury	Jupiter	Venus	Saturn	Sun	Moon
7:00 AM	Sun	Moon	Mars	Mercury	Jupiter	Venus	Saturn
8:00 AM	Venus	Saturn	Sun	Moon	Mars	Mercury	Jupiter
9:00 AM	Mercury	Jupiter	Venus	Saturn	Sun	Moon	Mars
10:00 AM	Moon	Mars	Mercury	Jupiter	Venus	Saturn	Sun
11:00 AM	Saturn	Sun	Moon	Mars	Mercury	Jupiter	Venus

	Sunday	Monday	Tuesday	Wednesday	Thursday	Friday	Saturday
Noon	Jupiter	Venus	Saturn	Sun	Moon	Mars	Mercury
1:00 PM	Mars	Mercury	Jupiter	Venus	Saturn	Sun	Moon
2:00 PM	Sun	Moon	Mars	Mercury	Jupiter	Venus	Saturn
3:00 PM	Venus	Saturn	Sun	Moon	Mars	Mercury	Jupiter
4:00 PM	Mercury	Jupiter	Venus	Saturn	Sun	Moon	Mars
5:00 PM	Moon	Mars	Mercury	Jupiter	Venus	Saturn	Sun
6:00 PM	Saturn	Sun	Moon	Mars	Mercury	Jupiter	Venus
7:00 PM	Jupiter	Venus	Saturn	Sun	Moon	Mars	Mercury
8:00 PM	Mars	Mercury	Jupiter	Venus	Saturn	Sun	Moon
9:00 PM	Sun	Moon	Mars	Mercury	Jupiter	Venus	Saturn
10:00 PM	Venus	Saturn	Sun	Moon	Mars	Mercury	Jupiter
11:00 PM	Mercury	Jupiter	Venus	Saturn	Sun	Moon	Mars

When working with planetary hours, the easiest thing is to simply work with each planetary energy on its own hour and on its own day - to work with Venus in the hour of Venus on Friday. However, this is not always possible. You may not be able to schedule an appropriate time on the appropriate day. You may not be able to wait until the appropriate day rolls around. It is also very common practice to do candle rituals as Novenas in which the rituals are repeated over multiple days. If you are going to do something like that, obviously, you are not going to be able to limit your work to that particular influence's day and perhaps not even to its hour. You have to find other compatible hours.

The following should give you an idea of what energies are generally compatible with which hours. (For rituals repeated over many days, the choice of the day is only important on the day you start. Starting in the correct hour, however, is important on each day that you work.) If you are not bothering with planetary hours, this will tell you which days of the week most favor work with which planetary energies. Once you do start working with hours, however, it is more important to select the appropriate hour than it is to select the appropriate day. If you are working with both days and hours, it is the correct hour that is crucial, the correct day is merely helpful. Even if you are working primarily with days, it might be helpful to know which hours of each day to avoid, although you don't have to memorize the exact reasons why.

I am not going to assign hours or days to the outer planets (Uranus, Neptune and Pluto), although some systems do. The planetary hour system I've given you may sound complicated at first but once you have it down, it will be very simple to work with. I don't want to hinder you by adding complexity. I will, however, tell you which hours are most compatible with the outer planets.

The Sun -   Most compatible with hours and days of Mercury, Venus, Mars and Jupiter.

The Moon -   Works well in the hours and days of Mercury, Venus and Jupiter.

Mercury -   Works well in the hours and days of the Sun, Venus and Jupiter.

Venus -   Works well in the hours and days of the Sun and Jupiter.

Mars -   Works best in the hours and days of the Sun and Jupiter and with Saturn's limiting energies.

Jupiter -   Works best with hours and days of the Sun and Venus.

Saturn -   Works best in his own hours only and his own day but possibly also with Mars.

Uranus -   Try Saturday or the hours of Saturn. Saturn and Uranus are two sides of the same coin. Many also recommend the "energetic" hour of Mars, but you have to be careful not to let Uranus build up too much steam. My instinct has always been to not be too fussy with Uranus and that any of the hours governed by pleasant, moderate energies like Venus or Mercury can work well, as can the dignifying, regulating energies of the Sun. It is the nature of Uranus to always be full of surprises, whatever hour you use, so select this energy only with caution. Saturn is really safest.

Neptune -   Works best in the hours and days of Jupiter, Venus and the Moon.

Pluto -   Works best on Tuesday and in the hours of Mars.

In general, be careful of using the hours Mars or Saturn for purposes for which they are not recommended. Mars is volatile. Saturn is limiting and tends to slow things down. His personality is, I suppose, best described as "cantankerous". Neither the Moon nor Mercury work well in these hours. Nor are the energies of Mars and Saturn known to work especially well in the hours of the Moon or Mercury.

Be careful also of Jupiter's tendency, despite his generally benevolent character, to make existing things increase. Saturn and Jupiter - limitation and expansiveness - make poor partners. Neither works well in the other's hour.

The hours and energies of the Sun and the Moon do not usually pair favorably. Venus and Mars are not the natural partners many might assume them to be, although the combination has limited uses in matters relating to sexuality.

With regard to the Outer Planets, exercise care when selecting an hour to work with Uranus because of his volatility and his tendency to bring sudden and radical change. As I said, this energy is not fussy but it is full of surprises. You usually have to temper Uranus with something. Make sure that it is appropriate to your purposes. A little of this energy goes a long way. (You don't really have to use Uranus all that often, anyway. If all you want is speed, use Mercury. If all you want is more mutability in a situation, use the Moon.) Keep in mind also that Neptune in an incompatible combination can cause sexual dysfunction or mental illness.

Ritual Design

Many of the books I have read on candle magic are filled with set ups for candle burning rituals for various purposes. They tell you what color candles to burn, what oil to dress them with, what incense to use and what words to say. There is little or no explanation of how these rituals were designed and very little that would help you create your own rituals. I have tried to give you something different here. I have tried to explain some principles you can use to create your own rituals. I have included not a lot of examples but a lot of guidelines and lots of options. The rituals may seem very elaborate. I fully expect that you will, eventually, streamline them. However, I would like you to streamline them in a way that makes sense to you. If, in a year or two, you are creating rituals which you feel to be effective, using only a single candle, that would be perfectly fine with me. You will also notice that I seldom tell you exactly what to say. I think that it is a good practice for you to write your own ritual formulas. This can include poems and hymns to the planetary influences and the angelic powers related to them.

It is also a good idea for you to keep a notebook, recording the rituals which you create and what results you think they had - even if this was only a change in the way you felt about things. You may limit this journal to ritual related material or make it a more general diary in which you record your thoughts, examine your intentions and discuss your interests. Remember, everything is interconnected. Nothing is irrelevant. Remember also that your own intuition about what works for you is central to the design of magical rituals for your use.

Invoking and Banishing Rituals

Invoking (Attracting) and Banishing rituals are the two basic kinds of magical rituals. Whatever you are doing, you are either trying to draw things into your life or drive them out of your life - or someone else's. Decide at the beginning which of these two basic operations you are attempting to perform. The candles then get "charged" either with oils or with carved symbols for the basic purpose of the ritual.

Charging with oil - Candles for invoking rituals get rubbed with oil from the top and bottom of the candle to the center of the shaft or clockwise around the top and or bottom of the candle. Candles for banishing rituals get rubbed with oil from the center of the shaft to the top and bottom of the candle or counter-clockwise around the top and or bottom of the candle. (In general gestures involved in invoking use motions drawing toward something and gestures involved in banishing involve motions pushing away from something.)

Charging candles with carvings or symbols - Candles for attracting should be carved with an invoking pentagram. Candles for banishing should be carved with a banishing pentagram. The appropriate planetary oils may be rubbed over these shapes in the direction the shape was carved.

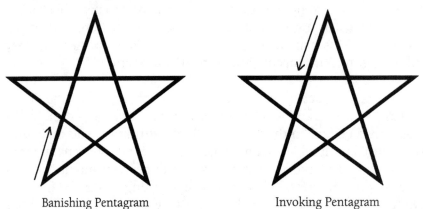

Banishing Pentagram   Invoking Pentagram

A basic thing that you should be aware of is that attracting something is the simpler and, therefore, the easier operation. Think of it this way: whatever you deal with in a magical ritual must first be made present in the ritual. Thus, you must make it manifest, even if you are only going to send it away. If you simply want something positive - like health or protection - to manifest, then the ritual is basically complete at that phase. However, if you want to get rid of something negative - disease, perhaps, or some threatening situation or person - the ritual has to progress to a second step of banishing that negative thing. The point here may be obvious: it's easier to work with attracting positive things like health and protection than it is to work with banishing negative things like disease or a threatening situation.

Banishing rituals, however, are very common and traditional. I am not suggesting that you not do them. (In fact, the blessing ritual that you perform over your candles before you use them is a banishing ritual.) I do suggest, however, that, in most cases, you design these rituals as composites. Don't just banish something negative. Also include operations to attract something positive in its place. Furthermore, don't design the ritual so that you constantly focus on or worry over the thing to be banished. Investing too much energy in a negative thing may make it more difficult, not easier to banish. Identify what it is, establish the fact that you want it to leave but then turn your attention to the good things that you want to replace it - imagine them forcing it out. Since we are working with candles, in practice this means that you extinguish the candle that represents the negative thing before the ritual ends. (The candles left burning at the end of the ritual should be those representing the forces you want to see triumph in the situation.) The rest of the ritual concentrates on attracting and strengthening the positive forces you want to replace the negative situation.

For example: you might burn an aqua candle (representing Neptune) if you wish to help someone overcome an addiction. You would also burn orange candles (representing the Sun) to draw health, vitality and courage into the person's life. The aqua candle would be extinguished first and then you would concentrate on attracting the positive forces the orange candles represents. Also, notice that I say aqua *candle* (singular) and orange *candles* (plural). It helps to have the candles representing the positive influence outnumber the candle representing the negative influence.

And remember, in banishing rituals, if you want to use Jupiter's influence, avoid lighting the candle that you have dedicated to Jupiter (purple or royal blue) until the candles representing negative forces are extinguished. Jupiter does signify good fortune but don't forget that it also signifies increase. If you are trying to banish something, you don't want it to increase! It's a good practice to wait until the ritual is completely devoted to things that you want to attract before lighting a Jupiter candle. (I wouldn't get overly obsessive about this, however. If you've got a purple candle on the altar for some other purpose - to represent a person born under the sign of Sagittarius, for example - or if you learn that your favorite incense has an ingredient in it that it is associated with Jupiter, it probably won't throw things off.)

I think I also ought to explain what exactly it is that I feel you are banishing. My personal theory is that we all have all the planetary influences operating in our lives all the time and that this is how things should be. The trick is to get them to operate appropriately. You are not banishing the planetary influence itself. You are banishing an unproductive aspect or a state of imbalance or disharmony in an area which the planetary influence governs. You should direct the planetary influence to help you remove the problem and to help you heal the situation. If you are using angelic powers, you should ask them to help, also. Think of the planetary influences and angelic powers as coming into harmony with your intentions and then escorting away something negative over which they exercise special control. Don't imagine them being themselves driven away or banished.

Healing Rituals

A very common type of ritual. For our purposes, I like to think that every ritual is, in some sense, a healing act. My only note here is to caution you that such rituals should be used to supplement whatever medical treatment the sick person has been instructed to undergo. Do not seek to be a substitute for medical science.

Here are some of the correspondences of the planetary influences to the different parts of the body. Generally, Venus (green candle) or the Sun (orange candle) is used for healing energy. You may wish to have a candle representing the afflicted part of system of the body or the nature of the affliction in the ritual. Knowing what planetary influence is involved will also mean that you can call on the planetary influence governing that specific part or system of the body to aid in the healing. Here's a sample of some traditional associations. (If you find that you are drawn to healing magic, research and your own intuition can give you a more precise understanding.)

The Sun -	The heart, the eyes, the upper back, growth, vitality.
The Moon -	Bodily fluids, birth and fertility, the stomach and lungs.
Mercury -	Nervous system and brain, cognition, speech, the waist, the hands.
Venus -	Internal sex organs, the kidneys, the veins, mouth and nasal passages, the neck and throat, hair, relaxation.

Mars -	Nose, ears, face, external sex organs, elimination, gall bladder, blood, energy level.
Jupiter -	Liver, the arteries, digestion, hips, thighs and feet.
Saturn -	Skin, bones and teeth, the spleen, the glands and the knees, anxiety.

For a healing ritual, you might try placing a candle representing the person to be healed (astrological sign) and a candle representing the afflicted area or the ailment on the altar. The ritual might end up with these candles surrounded by Venus and/or Sun candles, representing healing.

Love Rituals

As I have mentioned before, this is a very traditional type of ritual. Do not, however, ever seek to compel someone to love you or someone else. Do a ritual instead to draw love into your life in a general way - to increase your perception of opportunities to love and be loved and to your receptiveness to that love. You may also wish to perform a ritual to heal a relationship that has fallen into trouble. Here, you have to use your judgment. The relationship in question should be a long-standing committed relationship and should generally have been positive. It is best if one of the parties has asked for your help. Don't try to trap the parties in the relationship, however. Bless them. Try to help them find their love again. But state things in such a way as to leave them the option of parting their ways if that is really the best way for them to continue. Try to insure an amicable, peaceful parting if that must be.

A love ritual might be done by placing two candles representing the couple (by their astrological signs) side by side. The goal might be to surround them with Venus candles (pink) for love and possibly also Mercury candles (yellow) for communication. If you are trying to draw love into the life of a lonely person, the object might be to surround a candle representing the lonely person (by astrological sign) with pink Venus candles.

If you are trying to help someone meet his or her soulmate, you might do a ritual similar to the one for the couple. However, you would only use an astrological sign candle to represent the person who was known to you. The yet unknown soulmate might be represented by a silver candle if the person wished to acquire a female partner or a gold candle if the person preferred a male. The candles representing the couple would end up side by side surrounded by pink Venus candles and perhaps purple Jupiter candles (for good luck).

Ritual Structure

A ritual can be thought of like a story. It has a beginning, middle and an end. Indeed, the ancient Greek dramas had a religious, ritual function. A story also, of course, has a background situation that sets the tone for the events which unfold. So think of a ritual as being composed of four basic parts: Preparation, Opening, the Specialized Ritual, and Closing.

Preparation

Some people invest a great deal of preparation into their rituals. This is generally considered a good practice. There are others, however, who can just spontaneously grab a single, unprepared candle, light it, concentrate and say a few words and get wonderful results simply through visualization. For now, assume that you are the kind of person who needs to prepare. You will, over time, develop a preparation routine that works for you.

Preparing yourself - be well rested and generally well nourished, although eating a heavy meal immediately before a ritual may leave you tired. Many people bathe before doing a ritual and some make these baths very complicated affairs with special herbs, etc. Your hands, at least, should be clean. Many people have special clothing for ritual or change into clean clothes that have not been subjected to the activities and stresses of the day. Some do ritual work in the nude but if you are not used to ritual nudity or not comfortable with it, there is no reason to take it up for our system. It is important that your clothes are comfortable (and that they not have trailing sleeves or ornaments that might dangle in the candle flames and catch fire). It is also probably good for your clothes to be clean and fresh. You may wish to meditate or do a relaxation exercise before beginning. Also, start your visualization of white light as you collect your thoughts. Don't just see it, feel it move around you and through you. Let it radiate from you.

Preparing the space - the ritual space should be clean and neat, if possible. It helps to have a fresh and orderly environment in which to work. Remember, you are trying to order the cosmos - or at least your perceptions of it! For this reason, even if you are not normally a "neat freak", you may find chaotic surroundings very disturbing when you perform a ritual. If you use a sanctuary candle, light it before you begin. You may also light incense before starting, if you are going to use it.

Preparing the candles - if you are reusing candles, then their preparation begins when the ritual you last used them in ends. Using a soft cloth, rub them off with pure mineral oil when you clear the altar area. Rub in a motion away from you, to banish influences from the ritual. You may want to store them wrapped in a clean cloth and sorted by color. At a later time, clean them more thoroughly, trimming off drippings and straightening the shape with your ritual work knife. Scrape off any symbols carved in the wax. Dey recommends cleaning the wicks with alcohol. Rub them off again, once again using a motion away from you, this time you might want to use pine oil, known for its cleansing and protective powers or something else that appeals to you. You may then put the candles away again or use them. You may want to give new candles a similar cleaning.

Dey also recommends blessing the candles before using them. The following ritual is loosely based on what she describes. The sanctuary candle, if you use one, should be lit when you do this and the incense, if you are going to use it, should be burning. (Think of a few ritual words to say whenever you light this candle and words to say when you extinguish it. It should probably be something about blessing the space and purifying your intentions. If you use a bell, this might be a good time to ring it.) Place the candles which you are going to use for the ritual on the altar. You may wish to sprinkle them with some kind of sacred water - Dey lists prepared holy water, (there are Pagan holy water recipes) natural rain water and spring water as possibilities as well as water scented with something that appeals to you or has special significance. If you use a bell, you might ring it. You might call on the Holy Spirit, as Dey recommends, or possibly on the light of the Great Goddess or something else consistent with your religious tradition - perhaps simply the Pure Light of Divine Goodness or Wisdom. In your own words, ask that the candles be cleansed and blessed. Dey recommends that you draw a banishing pentagram over the candles or make the sign of the cross over them - three times. (She calls this cross a "solar cross" - a symbol far older and more universal that Christian cross symbolism.) Visualize them being flooded with white light. If you are using stick incense or have a hanging incense burner, you might want to pass the incense over the candles. Next, you cut any symbols into the candle you think are appropriate - astrological symbols, invoking or banishing pentagrams. (It is also possible to carve the symbols in the candles in advance.) Then you dress them with the oil for the appropriate planetary influences. Do this in the manner appropriate for the type of ritual you are going to do - attracting or banishing. Concentrate on the purpose of the ritual as you dress the candles. Continue to visualize white light radiating from them. Finally, you set the candles into their holders and position them for the beginning of the ritual. You are then ready for the opening phase of your ritual. (You may wish to use a similar procedure with other ritual objects. You may wish to bless your cutting knife and any other tools you use.)

Opening

I'm going to give you some basic features of the opening phases of a magical ritual. This will help you to design your own.

If you are using a sanctuary candle it should be lit before you start these operations.

The first step when performing a magical ritual is to establish a circle or protected, dedicated area. (This is especially true when working indoors - which is where candle rituals are generally performed.) Cunningham reports that a customary size for this area is a diameter of nine feet. That will not be possible in small spaces. If you have other people working with you, you may find you need more space.

What you need is a circle big enough to hold your altar table, with enough room for you to stand in front of it without feeling confined and enough room for the sanctuary candle (if you are using one) beside it.

First, I would establish the circle. This can be done by pointing with the athame and turning around to inscribe an imaginary circle on the floor around you and your work area - perhaps the best procedure if you don't have room to actually walk around the space. The motion for this operation should always be clockwise. There are other possible ways of accomplishing this, however. Some sources suggest very complicated operations for marking the ritual area off on the floor involving things like precisely drawn salt circles (done by trickling the salt out of the tip of a paper cone) with candles or symbolic objects marking the compass points. Cunningham suggests marking off the circumference of the circle with chalk, a cord, scattered shells or flowers petals or other appropriate seasonal material. He lists more exotic possibilities like a ring of tarot cards or crystals. He also suggests possibly playing ascending scales on a flute while walking around the area clockwise for further purification of the space. He suggests that if you are going to spread or scatter anything, you should hold it in your hand first and imagine it becoming energized. I would suggest that you visualize this energy as white light. My suggestion would be to simply walk clockwise around the circle with burning incense three times - you may not even need to mark it off. (Light this incense from the sanctuary candle if you are using one.) Compose a chant to recite during this operation establishing the area as a space where no harm shall be done and where nothing harmful should intrude.

The most important thing, however, it to visualize a wall of white light flowing from you (and from the sanctuary candle, if you have one) forming a protective wall or perhaps even a dome around your work area (and perhaps even extending around under the floor or earth beneath you). I told you at the beginning of the text to make a habit of visualizing a radiant white light. Try to imagine that it is this same white light radiating from every candle you light in the ritual. In practice, try to light every candle that you use from another candle so that all the flames are somehow the same flame.

After establishing the circle, I would light the two main altar candles, if you are using those. Do this by transferring flame with a small stick from the sanctuary candle, if you are using one.

A traditional part of an opening ritual is "calling the quarters". For some people, this is the same as casting the circle. Each of the four compass points represents one of the four mystical elements (Air, Fire, Water and Earth) and each has its own angelic power just as the planets do. You should create a statement acknowledging each of these directions, naming and thanking its element and asking the angelic power that represents it to watch and guard while you work. Whenever you invoke a power, you might ring a bell three times to indicate that it is manifest. You might also draw an invoking pentagram. Furthermore, even if you are not using the angelic powers associated with the planetary influences in the ritual, I would not omit the angels that represent the quarters. (Wiccan rituals often have symbols of the four quarters placed at the compass points or on the corners of the altar. In a candle ritual you probably have enough going on without worrying about these objects. Unless you are used to having them and like them, I would omit them.) Traditionally, you need only face the direction you are acknowledging as you call each quarter; basically, you just stand in place and turn to face each compass point. Since calling the quarters need not involve walking around the rear of the altar, you might decide to do this instead of casting the circle as described above, if space is limited. You should still visualize a protective barrier of white light forming a protective circle or dome around the area where you will be working.

The traditional correspondences of the quarters or four compass points are:

North -	Earth (element), Uriel (angel)
East -	Air (element), Raphael (angel)
South -	Fire (element), Michael (angel)
West -	Water (element), Gabriel (angel)

The traditional way of doing this seems to be to start by facing the North (Earth) and then proceed around the compass points in a clockwise direction facing East (Air) next, then South (Fire) and then West (Water). Many sources start in the East - and this may work better if you are using an East-facing altar. There, in fact, are a surprising number of different ways of performing this procedure. If you find a variation that works better for you, use it. After you have done this, light colored candles (or appropriate incense) representing the planet ruling the day and the planetary hour, if you are using those. Since the planetary hour can vary depending on the system you use to determine it, I would compose statements dedicating the day and the hour to the appropriate planetary influence and saying how you hope those particular influences will aid in the ritual. You may draw an invoking pentagram in the air as you speak the words or circle a pendulum in a clockwise direction over the candles and incense when you do this. You can ring the bell again, if you are using one, after each of these statements is made.

The Specialized Ritual

The Specialized Ritual (Invoking or Banishing) is the main body of the ritual. This is the place where the work gets done, the thing you have been preparing for and setting the stage for. This is the part that we really think of as "the candle magic ritual". You have been selecting candle colors for this phase, selecting the appropriate day and hour for this phase. This is the part where you must do most of the design.

There are several traditional procedures that can be used in this phase. The first is what we might call the "sympathetic magic" or "puppet theatre" method. In this, you manipulate the candles like puppets on a stage to show how you want to various planetary influences to effect different things and people.

For example, if you are trying to protect a friend from an enemy, you might do a banishing ritual to remove that enemy's influence from your friend's life. In the preparatory phase, you select a candle to represent the friend (astrological sign). You also select a candle to represent the enemy (astrological sign). Then you select a protective planetary influence - the Sun (orange candle) would be good. Let's say you want the enemy to be banished quickly so you decide that Mercury's influence (yellow candle) might also be helpful and include that as well. You mark, dress with oil and perhaps verbally identify these candles during the preparatory phase.

In the specialized phase of the ritual, you begin with the candles representing your friend and your enemy next to each other. The Sun candles (several) and Mercury candles (one or two) are lined up behind them. You light the candles representing the people first, stating who they represent. Dey also suggests that when you declare that a candle is supposed to represent a person, you pick the (unlit) candle up and blow on it - "breathing life into it", so to speak. Whenever you do this, you can ring the bell, if you are using one. Then you light the Sun candles, stating what they represent and what effect you want them to have. You might say something like: "I light this candle to protect my friend...[friend's name]...from all harm especially the designs and malice of ...[enemy's name]...". Then light the Mercury candles stating what they represent and what effect you want them to have: "I light this candle so that help may come quickly to...[friend's name]...". You then move the candles representing your friend and his or her enemy apart. You move the orange Sun candles between them and leave the yellow Mercury candles standing in place - "keeping watch", so to speak. You move the friend and enemy further apart. You place the Sun candles in a circle around the friend's candle. Then you extinguish the enemy's candle. (You can lift it off the table, blow it out and put it aside, for emphasis.) Leave the friend's candle, the Sun candles and the Mercury candles burning for the rest of the ritual. Throughout the different phases of the ritual you state - in words that you compose - what effect you wish your ritual actions to have in the real world, call on the different energies (in this case the Sun and Mercury) and ask the angelic powers (in this case Michael and Raphael) for their help. You may also read or recite appropriate psalms, other holy texts or even poems which you have written. It's like a puppet show that you hope to see reflected in real life.

The second method is similar. I would call it the "word and gesture method" because it depends more on what you say and do and less on moving candles around. Much here depends, however, on the order in which the candles are lit.

If we were adapting the banishing ritual described above for this method, you would begin with the candles placed with the Sun candles circles around the friend's candle and the enemy's candle off to the side. (Yes, this is very similar to the end position in the "puppet theatre" method of performing this ritual.) The Mercury candles would be "keeping watch" in the rear.

You light the friend's candle first, then the enemy's. You state who each of these candles represents as you are lighting them. If you are using a bell, you use it in this ritual just as you did in the one above, ringing it whenever you identify a candle with a person or an influence. You may also blow on the candles representing people before you light them, as in the ritual above. You can trace an invoking pentagram in the air as you light the friend's candle and a banishing pentagram when you light the enemy's. Or you can circle a pendulum in a clockwise direction around the friend's candle and in a counter-clockwise direction around the enemy's. That would be invoking and banishing respectively. When both are lit you state the problem and the outcome you desire. (You may wish to repeat the traced pentagrams or the pendulum circles over each candle.) Then you light the Sun candle and recite something that you have prepared calling down the influence of the Sun to protect your friend against their enemy and ask that the enemy's influence be banished. (This is where you would ring the bell.) Make either an invoking pentagram in the air or clockwise pendulum circles over each of the Sun candles as you do this. You might read or recite an appropriate psalm or other text. Then you light the Mercury candles and - in your own words - call down the influence of Mercury so that your friend might be helped quickly. (Ring the bell again, if desired.) Make the pentagram gestures or pendulum circles for the Mercury candles as you did for the Sun candles. Then you extinguish the candle representing the enemy after either tracing the banishing pentagram in the air or making a counter-clockwise pendulum circle over the candle before you do so. State your intention that malicious influences cease to trouble your friend.

You leave the friend's candle and the Sun and Mercury candles burning until the ritual is completed. As they burn, continue to recite and texts or speak any words that you feel are appropriate.

I tend to prefer this method because it requires less manipulation of burning candles. You can also probably use this method in a smaller space.

Obviously, elements of these two methods can be combined. Don't be afraid to be spontaneous. If you are inspired, for example, to draw the pentagrams when using the "puppet theatre" method, there is no reason why you should not do so. If you are using the "word and gesture" method and feel inspired to move the enemy's candle further and further from the friend's candle before extinguishing it, go right ahead.

Another type of ritual is the Novena. The name is taken from the Latin word for "nine". It refers to the Roman Catholic tradition of performing devotions over a period of nine days for the sake of a specific intention. For our purposes, it is simply a ritual repeated over several days. Three day, seven day and nine day rituals are all popular. You might use it with the "puppet theatre" method above, moving the candles into their final positions gradually over the course of several days.

Novenas, however, take their strength primarily from repetition. They can, therefore, be very simple. You don't have to use a lot of specialized candles. You might burn some incense and light a single dressed and marked colored candle, at an appropriate planetary hour, beginning on an appropriate day. You would say some words of your own over the candle, stating what you would like to see happen. You would repeat this process over the course of several days at an appropriate planetary hour. (There are even seven knobbed candles available in occult stores in a limited range of colors for use in seven day ritual cycles.)

It is a common practice to use psalms and biblical passages in candle rituals. Many of the psalms are actually quite ancient. Well, of course, the Bible is an ancient book but some of the psalms rank among the oldest texts in the Hebrew scriptures. As you would expect, many of these texts are original products of Hebraic culture and its various religions. The Israelites, however, were a semi-nomadic people and came in contact with many neighboring cultures. The religious poems we know as the psalms may derive from many different sources. Even if you don't use them, they can still serve as models for ritual words which you write. An alternative ancient practice, perhaps better suited to Pagan practitioners, would be to recite a mythic story that some how models the result you

would like to get from your ritual. Horus defeating Set, for example,
for victory over an enemy or Eros and Psyche in order to find true
love. (And, if you have no objection to Bible stories, parts of the
story of Jacob in Genesis might be good for prophetic dreams.) You
can integrate this procedure into whatever form of candle ritual you
like to use. Having a relevant mythic tale unfold over many days
while a ritual candle is burned, might make an interesting Novena.

Here's a list of some psalms, commonly used with candle rituals, and
the types of intentions they are used for:

Psalm 1 -   Protection, especially for the home.
Psalm 2 -   Protection from a slandering rival.
Psalm 3 -   Support against stress and malice.
Psalm 23 - Peace and healing. Good to start a ritual.
Psalm 25 - Peace, calm and enlightenment.
Psalm 26 - Self control and achievement.
Psalm 30 - Thanksgiving and protection.
Psalm 31 - Conquer fear.
Psalm 35 - Protection from danger, especially illness.
Psalm 36 - Protection from danger, especially gossip.
Psalm 38 - Protection of reputation and relief from illness or unwanted lust.
Psalm 39 - Courage and self-confidence especially against slander and mockery.
Psalm 41 - Help when betrayed or destitute.
Psalm 51 - Relief from guilty feelings.
Psalm 54 - Support against stress and malice.
Psalm 59 - Protection against powerful enemies.
Psalm 70 - Protection against malicious people.
Psalm 71 - Release from confinement and miserable conditions
Psalm 91 - For protection against many problems.
Psalm 93 - Protection from imprisonment, servitude or oppression.
            Good to start a ritual.
Psalm 95 - To overcome obstacles
Psalm 121 - Protection from mortal danger.
Psalm 128 - Peaceful home.
Psalm 130 - To summon help. Good to start a ritual.
Psalm 133 - To unite a family or group.
Psalm 134 - For dedication and studiousness.

For matters of love or to strengthen a marriage, it is traditional to select passages from the Song of Solomon.

To add Tarot cards to a ritual, first determine what planetary influences dominate the ritual and choose the Tarot cards associated with those planets. (Use the material on pages 43-44 to help you do this.) Then you may add other cards that help you focus on the desired outcome of the ritual, without regard to astrological correspondences. I've used only Major Arcana cards in these examples; you may, of course, add appropriate Minor Arcana cards.

To give you an idea of how Tarot cards might be used, here is an example of a Tarot ritual to bring insight through dreams. To select the proper cards begin first by asking: what planetary influence rules dreams and intuition? That would be the Moon. That planetary influence is represented with a white candle. The High Priestess is the card associated with the Moon. Its Hebrew letter is Gimel. Are there any Tarot cards that would help focus the ritual on dreams? The Moon card would. Its letter is Qoph. Now, we want communication through dreams not just dreams. Mercury is the planet of communication. Its color is yellow. Its card is the Magician and that card's letter is Beth. Is there any card that would help to further focus the ritual on communication? The Star would. Its letter is Tzaddi. So you would set up a candle ritual (following one of the methods whatever method you like) using white and yellow candles. To help with focus, you would lay out the Tarot cards: the High Priestess and the Magician. Beneath them you would place the Moon and the Star. You would carve the white candle with the astrological symbol for the Moon and the Hebrew letters Gimel and Qoph. The yellow candles would be carved with the symbol for Mercury and the letters Beth and Tzaddi. (The cards the Star and the Moon are associated with Aquarius and Pisces respectively, but we are not using those correspondences in the ritual because it will clutter things up.) You would also use a candle representing the person on whose behalf the ritual is being done by his or her astrological sign. You would also place the Minor Arcana court card most appropriate to that person in the center of the four other cards. The mystical characteristics of the Moon dominate the ritual. For this reason, you would probably want burn incense associated with the Moon. You may also want to choose a planetary hour or day of the week associated with the Moon's influence.

Or let us imagine that you would like to render an enemy's efforts ineffective. You would select a candle to represent the enemy by astrological sign and a court card from the Minor Arcana. Then you would ask what planetary influence you could use to represent the restriction you want to place on the enemy's behavior? That would be Saturn, of course. Its card is the World and the letter is Tau. The candle would be indigo. But is there a Tarot card that represents limitation or stagnation? That would be the Hanged Man. Its letter is Mem. In this ritual, you would be using indigo candles carved with the symbol for Saturn and the Hebrew letters Tau and Mem. (You wouldn't do anything with the Hanged Man's association with the mystical element of Water because it would complicate the ritual.) The cards would be arranged with the World above the court card representing the enemy and the Hanged Man below it. You might burn incense associated with Saturn and perform the ritual at a time compatible with the influence of Saturn.

I mentioned that you might try using rituals to ward off something signified by a negative card in a Tarot reading. To do this, you would surround a card and a candle representing the person for whom you did the reading with positive cards (perhaps positive cards that came up in the same reading) and surround those with orange candles representing the positive, protective energy of the Sun (or candles representing some other appropriate positive planetary influence). You might even partly cover the card representing the person with the Sun card. You would place the negative card outside this protective circle with a candle that somehow represents its destructive negative energy. You would then simply follow the instructions for a banishing ritual, removing the card representing the negative influence from the altar and extinguishing its candle.

Or if the card has a negative meaning because it is an otherwise positive card that came up in a reading upside down (if you are experienced with the Tarot, you will know which cards these are), then the ritual might involve turning the card right side up. This might be an interesting ritual because you would be working with an influence that is already there, and trying to change it from its negative to positive aspect. You could start with unlit candles representing some positive planetary energy and light them one at a time as you gradually turn the card right side up. Normally, we've been using the Sun but if the card represented stagnation, you might use Mercury for its association with speed. If it represented infertility or poverty, you might use Venus. You might even devise a ritual using seven candles and involving all seven planets, calling on each one in turn, by virtue of its own special attribute, to reverse the ill effects of the upside down card.

You may want to do another reading after this, perhaps using the card that you were trying to ward off or reverse as the starting card. This kind of reading may give you some advice as to how to proceed in order to bring the desired changes into effect.

Closing

It is traditional, when closing a candle ritual, to work backwards. In general, any candles that are still burning at the close of the ritual are extinguished in reverse of the order in which they were lit. (Candles representing negative forces or things to be banished should always be extinguished *first*, however. You should, at some point, be able to look at the altar and see only candles representing helpful, positive forces.) As you extinguish the planetary candles bid the planetary influences and angelic powers represented to go in peace. Ask them to watch over you and any on whose behalf the ritual was done. If you are using angelic powers, you might include a word of thanks in this closing message. Before you extinguish the main altar candles, similarly say farewell to the quarters. After you extinguish the main altar candles in your own words bid a general farewell to all the forces that have been present and bid them go in peace as you have been doing all along. Cunningham suggests that you imagine yourself absorbing the energy - in our case the white light - from the circle back into yourself. Declare your circle open in whatever way you think appropriate. After you rest for a bit, clean up the area with the sanctuary candle lit, if you use one. You may wish to sit and contemplate its light for a while when you are finished. Extinguish the sanctuary candle with any words or prayers you think fit.

DIAGRAMS

Banishing Ritual - "Puppet Theater" Method

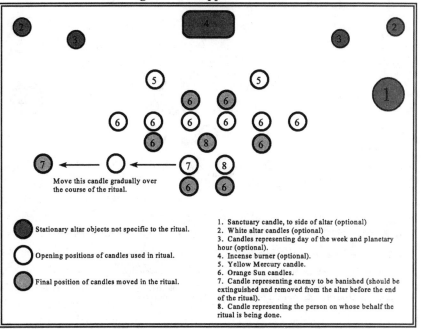

Move this candle gradually over the course of the ritual.

Stationary altar objects not specific to the ritual.

Opening positions of candles used in ritual.

Final position of candles moved in the ritual.

1. Sanctuary candle, to side of altar (optional)
2. White altar candles (optional)
3. Candles representing day of the week and planetary hour (optional).
4. Incense burner (optional).
5. Yellow Mercury candle.
6. Orange Sun candles.
7. Candle representing enemy to be banished (should be extinguished and removed from the altar before the end of the ritual).
8. Candle representing the person on whose behalf the ritual is being done.

Banishing Ritual - "Word and Gesture" Method

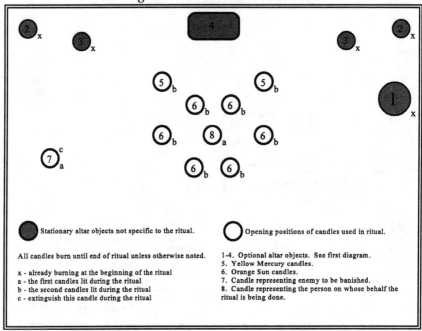

Stationary altar objects not specific to the ritual.

Opening positions of candles used in ritual.

All candles burn until end of ritual unless otherwise noted.

x - already burning at the beginning of the ritual
a - the first candles lit during the ritual
b - the second candles lit during the ritual
c - extinguish this candle during the ritual

1-4. Optional altar objects. See first diagram.
5. Yellow Mercury candles.
6. Orange Sun candles.
7. Candle representing enemy to be banished.
8. Candle representing the person on whose behalf the ritual is being done.

Healing Ritual - "Word and Gesture" Method

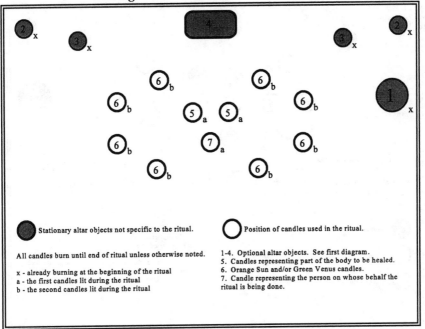

Stationary altar objects not specific to the ritual.

Position of candles used in the ritual.

All candles burn until end of ritual unless otherwise noted.

x - already burning at the beginning of the ritual
a - the first candles lit during the ritual
b - the second candles lit during the ritual

1-4. Optional altar objects. See first diagram.
5. Candles representing part of the body to be healed.
6. Orange Sun and/or Green Venus candles.
7. Candle representing the person on whose behalf the ritual is being done.

Soulmate Ritual - "Puppet Theater" Method

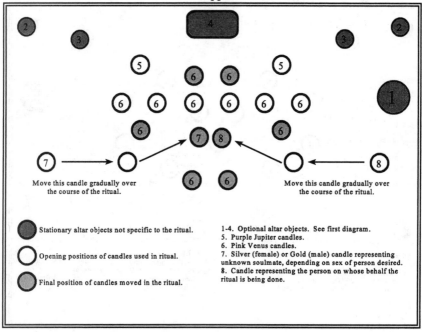

Move this candle gradually over the course of the ritual.

Move this candle gradually over the course of the ritual.

Stationary altar objects not specific to the ritual.

Opening positions of candles used in ritual.

Final position of candles moved in the ritual.

1-4. Optional altar objects. See first diagram.
5. Purple Jupiter candles.
6. Pink Venus candles.
7. Silver (female) or Gold (male) candle representing unknown soulmate, depending on sex of person desired.
8. Candle representing the person on whose behalf the ritual is being done.

Banishing the Influence of an Unfavorable Tarot Card

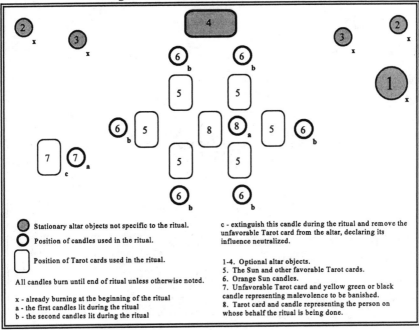

Stationary altar objects not specific to the ritual.

Position of candles used in the ritual.

Position of Tarot cards used in the ritual.

All candles burn until end of ritual unless otherwise noted.

x - already burning at the beginning of the ritual
a - the first candles lit during the ritual
b - the second candles lit during the ritual

c - extinguish this candle during the ritual and remove the unfavorable Tarot card from the altar, declaring its influence neutralized.

1-4. Optional altar objects.
5. The Sun and other favorable Tarot cards.
6. Orange Sun candles.
7. Unfavorable Tarot card and yellow green or black candle representing malevolence to be banished.
8. Tarot card and candle representing the person on whose behalf the ritual is being done.

Tarot Ritual - Reversing an Unfavorable Card

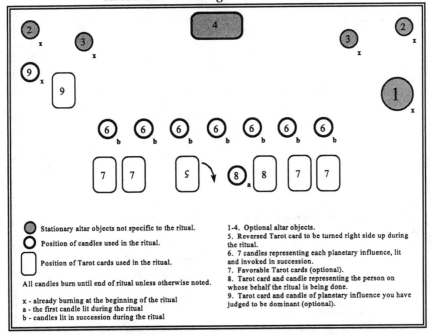

Stationary altar objects not specific to the ritual.

Position of candles used in the ritual.

Position of Tarot cards used in the ritual.

All candles burn until end of ritual unless otherwise noted.

x - already burning at the beginning of the ritual
a - the first candle lit during the ritual
b - candles lit in succession during the ritual

1-4. Optional altar objects.
5. Reversed Tarot card to be turned right side up during the ritual.
6. 7 candles representing each planetary influence, lit and invoked in succession.
7. Favorable Tarot cards (optional).
8. Tarot card and candle representing the person on whose behalf the ritual is being done.
9. Tarot card and candle of planetary influence you have judged to be dominant (optional).

Tarot Ritual to Bring Dreams

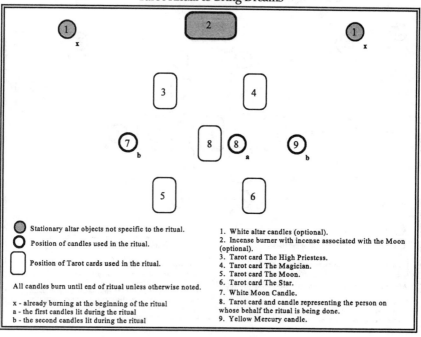

Stationary altar objects not specific to the ritual.

Position of candles used in the ritual.

Position of Tarot cards used in the ritual.

All candles burn until end of ritual unless otherwise noted.

x - already burning at the beginning of the ritual
a - the first candles lit during the ritual
b - the second candles lit during the ritual

1. White altar candles (optional).
2. Incense burner with incense associated with the Moon (optional).
3. Tarot card The High Priestess.
4. Tarot card The Magician.
5. Tarot card The Moon.
6. Tarot card The Star.
7. White Moon Candle.
8. Tarot card and candle representing the person on whose behalf the ritual is being done.
9. Yellow Mercury candle.

Tarot Ritual to Stop an Enemy

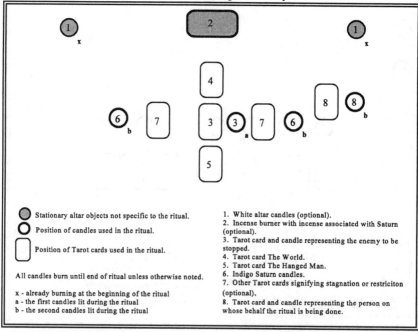

Stationary altar objects not specific to the ritual.

Position of candles used in the ritual.

Position of Tarot cards used in the ritual.

All candles burn until end of ritual unless otherwise noted.

x - already burning at the beginning of the ritual
a - the first candles lit during the ritual
b - the second candles lit during the ritual

1. White altar candles (optional).
2. Incense burner with incense associated with Saturn (optional).
3. Tarot card and candle representing the enemy to be stopped.
4. Tarot card The World.
5. Tarot card The Hanged Man.
6. Indigo Saturn candles.
7. Other Tarot cards signifying stagnation or restriciton (optional).
8. Tarot card and candle representing the person on whose behalf the ritual is being done.

BOOKS FOR FURTHER
STUDY AND REFERENCE

This is a list of books that may prove helpful for those seeking to work with candle burning rituals. The information in these books may not always agree with what I have presented in this guide - indeed these resources can differ very strongly with each other! I encourage you to evaluate all material in terms of what works best for you. Also, I have listed some books here for reference purposes. I would caution you that books about magical lore often fail to acknowledge the existence of alternative customs or procedures. Compare references, seek to constantly improve your knowledge and take nothing as gospel.

Raymond Buckland, *Practical Candleburning Ritual*, (Llewellyn, 1993). Concentrates on examples of rituals rather than principles of ritual design. First published in 1970, this book has the very interesting feature of presenting both Christian and Pagan forms of the same ritual. Probably one of the most readily available books on candle magic at this time.

Paul Foster Case, *The Tarot: A Key to the Wisdom of the Ages*, (Macoy, 1975). Of all the more advanced and esoteric works on the mystical significance of the Tarot, this reprint of a 1947 work is probably one of the easiest to understand.

Richard Cavendish, *A History of Magic*, (Arkana, 1987). Exactly what the title says it is. It begins promisingly with the words "magic is as old as man", moves on through ancient Rome and ends up with Jung and the modern occult explosion. It may get a bit vague and simplistic when dealing with modern movements but, otherwise, seems to be a fascinating quick overview.

Scott Cunningham, *Wicca: A Guide for the Solitary Practitioner*, (Llewellyn, 1988). The Wiccan religion has a strong tradition of creative magical ritual. This is a gentle, very basic primer for those working without a group or an instructor. The second volume in the series is *Living Wicca*.

Scott Cunningham, *Cunningham's Encyclopedia of Magical Herbs*, (Llewellyn, 1985). A very thorough encyclopedia of herbal magic.

Melita Denning & Osborne Phillips, *Planetary Magick*, (Llewellyn, 1989). The authors' magical system aside, this reference work contains a great deal of lore, both basic and extremely esoteric, about the various planets and their influences. I would recommend further study in the principles of ceremonial magic and Qabala before really using this system or some of the more obscure information, but it contains so much food for thought about its subject that it can't be omitted here.

Charmaine Dey, *The Magic Candle*, (Original Publications, 1982). You'll probably have trouble getting this one but I must mention it. This rather low budget production was a very sincere, basic and thorough introduction to contemporary candle burning folk traditions.

Eden Gray, *A Complete Guide to the Tarot*, (Bantam, 1972). Originally published in 1970, this classic of popular occultism is a very clear and basic guide to the Tarot. It also contains simple introductions to several occult systems. It has some flaws, but this is the first book I would recommend for an absolute beginner with no knowledge of astrology, numerology or Qabala.

Marian Green, *A Witch Alone*, (Aquarian, 1991). Another Wiccan primer on magical ritual and religious values. It takes a creative approach and contains a good deal of original thinking about basic rituals. It is intended - as the title indicates - for people working alone.

Rosemary Ellen Guiley, *The Mystical Tarot*, (Signet, 1991). There are many paperback Tarot primers. This one, by a respected popular occult writer, offers very good information on the background and symbolism of the cards.

Gareth Knight, *Magic and the Western Mind*, (Llewellyn, 1991). A very interesting and intelligent basic history of European occultism and the philosophies behind it. First published in 1978 as *A History of White Magic*.

John Lust, *The Herb Book*, (Bantam, 1974). Another very thorough encyclopedia of herbal lore.

Marvin Meyer and Richard Smith, *Ancient Christian Magic: Coptic Texts of Ritual Power*, (Harper Collins, 1994). Something completely different. This is a scholarly collection of magical formulas and recipes from late antiquity. This often primitive and weird array illustrates what magical ritual was really like "in the wild": how it was constructed, what purposes it was used for, who used it, its relation to religion etc. - quite a change from our tidy, modern, magical primers.

Silver Ravenwolf, *To Ride a Silver Broomstick*, (Llewellyn, 1993). Another Wiccan primer, this one packed with many useful bits of information. The author has a strong and engagingly opinionated personality. Whether you always agree with her philosophy or not, there is a great deal in here of value, some of it geared specifically to candle magic.

Janina Renee, *Tarot Spells*, (Llewellyn, 1990). A useful book on using Tarot spreads to influence events rather than simply predict them. This book is also a good magical primer with some information on the use of colors and candles.

Anna Riva, *Candle Burning Magic*, (International Imports, 1980). An extensive guide to the folk magic rituals associated with candle burning both benign and aggressive. It evenhandedly includes some so-called "black magic" as well as information on Catholic veneration of saints and other Christian elements. Very thorough and interesting, if you happen across it, but offers little ethical guidance about the practices described.

Starhawk, *The Spiral Dance*, (Harper, 1979). This is the classic book of feminist oriented Wicca. It's included here because it contains examples of truly awesome rituals.

Jim Tester, *A History of Western Astrology*, (Boydell Press, 1987). Another good history. Not light reading, however, and probably only for those who are deeply interested in astrology. Only covers material up to the Enlightenment.

Leo Vinci, *The Book of Practical Candle Magic*, (Aquarian, 1981). Here is one of the classics of the tradition, if you can find it! It is a superbly intelligent introduction to the planetary system and treats candle burning magic as a dignified and sophisticated occult technique.

Arthur Edward Waite, *The Pictorial Key to Tarot*, (U.S. Games, 1983). This a reprinting of Waite's 1910 classic, explaining his understanding of the Tarot.

"Knowledge of correspondences was the chief of all knowledges... for the knowledge of corresponden- ces is angelic knowledge.... Without a knowledge of correspondence there can be no knowledge of the spiritual world or its inflow into the natural world.... The whole natural world corresponds to the spiritual world and not merely the natural world in general but every particular of it...."

- Emmanuel Swedenborg